I don't have to dwell on the point that cars mean more to these
kids than architecture did in Europe's great formal century, say,
1750 to 1850. They are freedom, style, sex, power, motion, color
– everything is right there.

Tom Wolfe, *The Kandy-Kolored Tangerine-Flake Streamline Baby*, 1964

First published in 2009 by Conran Octopus Ltd,
a part of Octopus Publishing Group,
2–4 Heron Quays, London E14 4JP UK
www.octopusbooks.co.uk

An Hachette UK Company
www.hachette.co.uk

Distributed in United States and Canada by Octopus
Books USA, c/o Hachette Book Group USA,
237 Park Avenue, New York, NY 10017 USA

Publisher: Lorraine Dickey
Managing Editor: Sybella Marlow
Copy Editor: Sian Parkhouse

Art Direction and Design: Jonathan Christie
Photographer: Tif Hunter
Photographer's Producer: Sue Allatt
Picture Researcher: Anne-Marie Hoines

Production Director: Frances Johnson
Production Manager: Katherine Hockley

ISBN: 978 1 84091 535 8
Printed in China

CARS

FREEDOM
STYLE
SEX
POWER
MOTION
COLOUR
EVERYTHING

STEPHEN BAYLEY

ORIGINAL PHOTOGRAPHY BY TIF HUNTER

Everywhere,
Giant finned cars nose forward like fish;
A savage servility
Slides by on grease.

Robert Lowell, *For the Union Dead*, 1964

Automobiles are hollow, rolling sculpture. They have interior spaces corresponding to an outer form, like buildings, but the designer's aesthetic purpose is to enclose the functioning parts of an automobile, as well as its passengers, in a package suggesting directed movement along the ground.

Arthur Drexler, 1951

This is not a book about cars.

At least, not in the sense of technology, production engineering, environmental impact, or motor racing. It is not about industry or manufacturing. You will find no references to power outputs, speed, acceleration… nor hardly any to cost. My subject is the more elusive one of art.

Because, ultimately, it was art that really made the car America's primary product. And later Europe's, then Japan's. The management consultancy pioneer, Alfred McKinsey, believed everything can be measured and if you can measure it, you can manage it. But art is as notoriously resistant to both measurement and management as it is powerful in its effect. From the moment car manufacturers discovered art in the 1920s, there have been attempts to manage it, to systematize it, but none has been successful. Even in an industry as hierarchical and stratified as automobile manufacturing, the great cars have been products of creative genius – aberrant, cussed, irreverent – not of scientific management.

This is a book about the 80 or so greatest car designs ever, the ones that changed conventional wisdom, lifted the game, raised the bar. At five minutes to midnight for the heat engine, it is a book with an elegiac quality since it was the very opportunities and constraints offered by Karl Otto's four-stroke cycle that established the architecture of that wonderful, unique expression of human genius we know as 'the car'. The suck-bang-

Introduction
Nature builds no machines

Opposite: **Car design turns raw materials into a means of expression. Renault's steel stockyard was photographed by company photographer Robert Doisneau, in 1935. Soon, billets and sheets will become sculpture.**

squeeze-blow of the Otto cycle will soon be history, but its legacy is still here to be enjoyed. Nothing, not even a building, has more passion, expertise and cunning put into its design.

This is a book about cars that were produced in series (even if, in the case of some Ferraris and Lamborghinis, that series was very short and relied to a large extent on craft techniques). This is a book about cars as the ultimate product of consumerized industrial capitalism. It is about mass production. Le Corbusier said mass production leads to standards, and standards lead to perfection.

By about 1901, the fundamental architecture of the car had been established by Daimler's 'Mercedes'. There were four wheels. There were usually four passengers, one of them behind the wheel (although at the very first it was a tiller). One of Dr Otto's internal combustion engines was mounted front or rear. Sometimes there might be just two passengers. The bodywork might be open, like a buggy, or closed like a state coach. Over the years shown in this book, this nearly inflexible architecture has inspired astonishing formal inventiveness by designers. Within a grid as fixed as the classical orders, metal (and occasionally, plastic) has been hammered, bent, pressed, stretched, perforated, chromed and painted in pursuit of emotional expression. People who say 'all cars tend to look the same' are people who do not have eyes to see. The variety and ingenuity astonishes while, commensurately, the disciplines are intense. Car designers learn to work within astonishing constraints, not just of technology, but of aesthetics, too. There is only a few millimetres' difference, Jaguar designer Geoff Lawson once explained, between a curve that is fat and a curve that is anorexic. Car designers have learnt a potent formal language: how one radius can convey strength, another weakness. They learn also about meaningful detail, the psychology of colour, proportion and the way light falls on surfaces. And they pass on these lessons to consumers.

Like all other designers, only more so, the car designer has to live in the future. This means, in effect, that when a brand-new car appears on the market, the designers have probably already designed the successor of its successor. The car designer's task is to dream, but in a practical way: he deals in fantasies measurable in millimetres and anchored by budgets and fickle consumer whim.

One of the founders of the industrial design profession was Raymond Loewy (whose postwar Studebaker Starliner had an influence wildly out of proportion to its commercial significance). Loewy liked to talk about the MAYA principle, or 'Most Advanced Yet Acceptable'. Ever since, car designers constantly test these limits. Sometimes, as with Patrick Le Quément's Renault Avantime, they create a vehicle of audacious conceptual originality which fails because it tests the public t oo much. But the most successful cars have the MAYA principle in correct balance… leaving just

Cars, cars, fast, fast! One is seized, filled with enthusiasm, with joy… the joy of power. The simple and naive pleasure of being in the midst of power, of strength.
Le Corbusier, *The City of Tomorrow*, 1929

enough room for next year's model. 'Go all the way and then come back some,' Harley Earl told his designers in Detroit. Very often they did not bother to come back much, as the '59 Cadillac shows. What fascinates is the extreme of human creativity.

'Detroit' means 'straight', although nothing could be more overwrought or visually complicated than Detroit's primary product at its economic peak. The '59 Cadillac is an engineering atrocity, viewed in the terms that, say, Dr Porsche would understand. Yet to admonish its designers for their head-butting assault on the environment is as sensible as reprimanding a fish for being wet. The '59 Cadillac was created in a world where Americans (at least) knew no constraints of appetite. The Germans called the phenomenon 'Detroit Machiavellismus'. But as Machiavelli insisted, the end result was what mattered, even if the end result was cruising down the freeway in a bright pink Cadillac.

The car is *the* most significant manufactured object. In America the automobile became, in a country where invention became the mother of necessity, a useful demonstration of Nathaniel Hawthorne's principle that wealth is the only true measure of rank. In Europe, with its more nuanced class system, cars were a measure of something other than wealth. Indifference is not an option. The person who declares, 'I'm not interested in cars, I just drive an old Volvo' is confirming what a statement a Volvo makes, especially if it has acquired the automobile equivalent of bottle age.

Above: The car gave freedom to consumers hitherto confined to urban life. At the same time, it altered for ever the relationship between town and country. Robert Doisneau's picturesque 'Déjeuner sur l'herbe', 1935.

Below: Even in the computer age, car designers use sculptural techniques a medieval mason would have recognized. A designer in Wolfsburg is working on a clay model of the Volkswagen Polo, 1984.

The evolution of car design is a story of fantastic artistry and inventiveness. Within the constraints of the architecture of the automobile, its wheels, seats and engine, metal and plastic and glass have been teased and tormented. It is a story of how the disparate forms of the horseless carriage became integrated into a whole. Then the story rapidly evolves so that the sculptural whole both interprets and, later, directs consumer psychology. As soon as car designers had, circa 1927, come to discover the sculptural possibilities of the mass-produced car, it was a moment of culture change. Only rock music and movies can compare with the cultural impact of the designed automobile.

Besides the sculptural inventiveness which made the consumer's cupidity itch, there is the philosophical idea of personal mobility embodied by the car. Ideas about mobility are fundamental to the liberal democracies where the car first flourished. This germ of freedom may be ineradicable from our

No dignity without chromium
No truth but a glossy finish
If she purrs she's virtuous
If she hits ninety she's pure…
William Carlos Williams, *Ballad of Faith*, 1954

understanding of what a car is (even as day-to-day conditions from Bangkok to Los Angeles mock the genie of freedom whom Henry Ford helped escape from his bottle on a Michigan farm).

When the Paris savant Roland Barthes made popular culture the subject of serious academic study he was aware of how the car acquired extraordinary symbolic power. In the greatest essay on the automobile written by a European, Barthes said of the Citroën DS (in *Mythologies*,

1957) 'cars are our cathedrals'. His intention was mischievous, but it was a serious observation. As technical achievements and as symbols of collective aspirations, churches of the Middle Ages and twentieth-century cars had much in common.

Seven years after Barthes, Tom Wolfe had another insight into the symbolic power of the car. Visiting a California drag strip, he realized Ford and Chevrolet were doing what Le Roi Soleil did at Versailles. Cars, Wolfe says, are tied up with

Opposite: The romance of the car was enhanced by celebrity accidents. James Dean's at the wheel of a Porsche RSK just a few days before his death in a 1955 collision with a Ford truck in the California desert.

Above: Photographers often responded to the physical qualities of fine cars with their gorgeous shapes and lustrous sheens. This is Louis Faurer's abstract study of Cadillacs in a Park Avenue garage, New York, 1950.

religion and architecture, just like sculpture in the age of Benvenuto Cellini. In *The Kandy-Kolored Tangerine-Flake Streamline Baby,* he wrote, 'Cars mean more to these kids than architecture did in Europe's great formal century, say, 1750 to 1850. They are freedom, style, sex, power, motion, color – everything is right there.' There you have my title.

The story of car design begins in 1908, which Aldous Huxley called 'The Year of our Ford'. Germans and Austro-Hungarians may have developed the technology of the car, but Henry Ford knew how to exploit it. The ordinary man's yearning for independence and freedom was the basis of his appeal. Ford was an epochal figure: an intuitive mechanical genius, a wizard of motivation, a plain-talking anti-Semite and anti-intellectual, a man obsessed with technology, but sentimentally located in small-town America of the nineteenth century. Henry Ford's cars eased Americans 'through the dislocations created by breathtaking

historical change', according to Steven Watts in his book *The People's Tycoon* (2005). Ford was obsessed by process, not art. His company had a (pioneering, if sinister) sociological department and Ford said, 'We want to make men in these factories as well as cars.' The term 'Fordism' was coined to describe this totalitarian approach to labour (the very approach that drew Hitler to Ford).

If the Ford achievement was in consumerizing mobility, its rival General Motors' achievement was in consumerizing dreams. There was a time before cars were designed, but then came Harley Earl. This extraordinary personality was the first person to realize that cars went from A to Z, not merely to B. Earl made cars sexy, among other attributes.

Thus it was Earl who gave the world some of its most potent modern symbols: the Detroit automobile of the high Fifties. These were cars to cruise in, although better adapted in many ways to the drive-in than to driving. Voluptuous curves,

Above: The Citroën 2CV – Pierre Boulanger's 'umbrella on wheels'.

Right: Zoltan Glass was an experimental Hungarian photographer who worked for Mercedes-Benz in the 1930s. His promotional photographs often used daring angles and radical compositions.

Opposite left: In America the automobile became a symbol of freedom as well as the consumer's alienation in a branded, mechanized world. 'All roads lead West' suggests a vista of endless possibility for this Buick.

Opposite right: The boat tail of a Mercedes-Benz Cabriolet photographed by Zoltan Glass at a Berlin Motor Show circa 1934. Hitler used the technocratic prestige of Mercedes-Benz as nationalist propaganda.

opulent paint, strange glass, lascivious chrome, pleated Naugahyde, bizarre symbolism. Yes, they were also cart-sprung barges with atrociously inefficient engines and no brakes. But if you can look at a '59 Cadillac, or even a humbler '59 Chevrolet Impala hardtop coupé (in Sunburst Yellow) and not wonder at the sheer, inflammatory wonder of it all, then you are reading the wrong book.

By raiding every iconographic source he could find, from fighter aircraft to rocket ships, the Santa Monica Raceway and rumba dancing, Earl gave form to the most vivid version of the American dream: a life made perfect by advanced consumerism. It is short-changing genius to say all he achieved was chrome baubles and tail fins. He gave America a mirror of its own ambitions.

Harley Earl was born in Hollywood on 22 November 1893, the son of J.W. Earl, a local coachbuilder. The Earls were prosperous, socially established and in a position to predict the coming

of the private car, an event anticipated by the relaunch in 1908 of the family business as the Earl Automobile Works. The company started making custom-made car bodies and fuselages for the Glen L. Martin Company, pioneers of Californian aerospace. Harley Earl's name first appeared in the newspapers in 1919 when the *Los Angeles Times* noted his spectacular bodywork at the local Auto Show. In these early designs, motifs that would later preoccupy Earl began to appear: he had an obsession about cars being ever longer, ever lower. He enjoyed sculpted transitions, not sharp abutments. The 'trunk' was once exactly that, a survivor from the days of the carriage trade: Earl did away with strap-on storage and integrated the boot into the body. He liked expressive details and he simply loved colour. While Henry Ford was mass-producing cost-effective black, Earl had a comedian client pour cream in his coffee until it reached exactly the desired shade of brown.

Drive ten thousand miles across America and you will know more about the country than all the institutes of sociology and political science put together.
Jean Baudrillard, *America*, 1989

When Don Lee, the West Coast Cadillac distributor, bought the Earl Automobile Works, it gave Earl a direct contact with Alfred Sloan's new conglomerate of General Motors. This organization was a masterpiece of American capitalist improvization. General Motors' twin objectives of profit and growth were established (and never questioned) by founders Sloan and his partners William C. Durant and Charles F. Kettering. From the Hyatt Roller Bearing Company and Guardian Frigerator Company grew GM's Detroit factoryscape and its five divisions, the first challenger to Ford's market dominance.

Earl was lured to the mid-West by Lawrence Fisher of the Cadillac Division. Alfred Sloan had mused about styling in 1921 and by 1926 the idea that the appearance of cars might actually affect sales was beginning to ripen. One of the weapons GM used to attack Ford was market segmentation: Ford thought a single product would suffice, Sloan disagreed. Thus Earl's first job was to fill an ugly $1,700 gap between Buick and Cadillac. This appeared in March 1927 under the new brand of La Salle and caused a sensation. Although inspired by the coachbuilt Hispano-Suiza (which Earl called 'Hisso'), to American eyes its appearance was entirely new: sharp corners had been excluded in favour of curved junctions, disparate elements were unified into a pleasing whole and the entire silhouette had been lowered to express speed and suggest elegance. Later, Earl said that his

Above: The influential 'Eight Automobiles' exhibition ran at New York's Museum of Modern Art in 1951. Curated by Arthur Drexler, it gave the world the expression 'rolling sculpture' and legitimized car design as an art form.

Below: Talbot-Lago T150SS, 1941. Unconstrained by cost and the technical disciplines of mass-production, coachbuilders such as Figoni & Falaschi were able to design astonishing shapes for one-off, handmade production.

first GM car was 'slab-sided, top heavy and stiff shouldered', but that was another way of saying how far he had travelled to reach the '59 Cadillac.

Thrilled by popular response to La Salle, Sloan now decided to acquire the transmutational services of Harley Earl for all GM divisions. On 23 June 1927 (the very same year that Raymond Loewy opened shop in Manhattan and started streamlining pencil sharpeners), Sloan announced the creation of the Art and Color Section with Harley Earl at its head. Just as the paint was drying on the Art and Color signage, Ford's Model T went out of production. The story of popular car design had begun. Art and Color's first car, the 1929 'pregnant' Buick, was not a success, but it taught Earl one of his great organizing principles: you have to lead the public, but not by too much. This was what Loewy had called MAYA.

A contemporary industrial innovation provided designers with a fresh canvas and extended Earl's personal vocabulary of form: US Steel introduced the high-speed strip which by 1934 was providing sheet metal in 2.2m (7ft 4 in) widths. Suddenly, new sculptural possibilities were viable. Three years later, Earl renamed Art and Color 'Styling' and, thus, a new word entered the vocabulary of international business. Styling's first job was to invent 'dream cars', drivers of the US economy, avatars of desire. A GM sales committee paper of 1925 had established the need for an annual model change to keep demand moving and it was Earl's job to lure the consumer with new visual ideas. To its critics this became planned obsolescence, but to GM it was more positively known as the dynamic economy. The first dream car was the 1937 Buick Y Job. Like everything else credited to Earl, it was actually drawn by someone else (in this case George Snyder), but it was part of Earl's innovative method to realize his creative vision by a process of critique, recommendation and, quite often, intimidation. Draftsmen trembled when he toured the studios.

Passenger car production stopped in the Second World War, but Earl's vaulting imagination was not hindered by the diversion of global conflict. GM's Allison Division supplied engines to Lockheed, whose P-38 was one of the most formally inventive and radical aircraft shapes. In 1942 Earl and his staff viewed one. Although not allowed any closer than 9m (30ft), it was enough. The projectile nose, the cockpit greenhouse, the beautifully contoured fuselage and (especially) the twin tail booms: Earl had found the source of car styling for the next decade. Those booms inspired vestigial tail fins on the '48 Cadillac. Oldsmobile followed in '49, Buick in '52, Chrysler in '55. Ford held out on tail fins until 1957, but by '59 the GM tail fin had evolved to the fantastical excess of the Impala. By the time Earl's tail fins had trickled down from the apex of Cadillac to the base of Chevrolet, in full conformity with the laws of planned obsolescence the Cadillac of the following year appeared as a model of restraint.

Two generations of Americans know more about the Ford coil than the clitoris, about the planetary system of gears than the solar system.

John Steinbeck, *Cannery Row*, 1945

Harley Earl invented the practices still used today: concept cars shown at presentations called 'Motoramas', clay modelling, platform sharing and brand separation. He called design 'thinking out loud' and insisted that the designer's role was to give the customer a 'visual receipt' for his dollars.

As cars became cleaner and more reliable, woman became involved. First as customers (who were promised temporary liberation from dream kitchens), then, in a bizarre before-its-time episode, as designers. WASPS to a woman, these Vanderbilts and Fords were Earl's 'Damsels of Design'. One Ruth Glennie did a Corvette which with pre-Freudian naivety she called 'Fancy Free' with silver, olive and white leather trim and slip covers to change with the seasons. Jeanette Linder had fitted fibreglass luggage in her Chevrolet Impala, pastel-striped to match the upholstery. Not satisfied with the manufacturer's ample provision of names for the Cadillac Eldorado Seville, Sue Vanderbilt proposed a Baroness version in subdued colours to 'permit the occupant to shine'. It had a black mouton carpet, a telephone and black seal-fur pillows and lap robe for rear passengers.

Never has a designer had as much power and influence and profile as Harley Earl. He wore cinnamon and sky blue linen suits, and kept changes of clothes in his office. He flew on the inaugural flight of the Boeing 707 and was filmed eating a banana. At design reviews he would lounge in chairs and point to details with the toe cap of a highly polished wingtip loafer. People said he lived as if auditioning for the role of the most unforgettable person you ever met. He had an absolute genius for automobile art. He died in 1969.

Europe had no equivalent to Harley Earl and General Motors, and car design there developed rather differently. The best European manufacturers and designers tended to be more concerned with the explicitly artistic and creative aspects of car design. Few companies have enjoyed a better reputation for design excellence, not to say wanton eccentricity, than Citroën. From the start, Andre Citroën invested creative beliefs and ideals in his manufacturing business. While this often frustrated conservative investors and bankers (resulting in bankruptcy in 1934), it also eventually produced what is, perhaps, the single most magical car design of them all: the Citroën DS.

Citroën's belief was that 'Dès l'instant qu'une idée est bonne, le prix n'a pas d'importance.' He also attached special significance to sales and promotion, which he turned into as vigorous an art form as car design itself. In the Citroën showroom on Paris' Champs-Elysées cars were given the reverence due to museum pieces. After the bankruptcy, the tyre supplier Michelin, a leading creditor, acquired the company. Citroën, a gambler in all aspects of life, died disappointed and broke one year later, but not before his principles had established a creative culture that led to a series of the most audacious designs ever seen.

We shall learn to be masters rather than servants of nature.

Henry Ford, 1922

Right: The style of a country's roads reflects a nation's preoccupations as accurately as the cars that drive upon them. This is America's Pacific Coast Highway, US1: vast, magnificent, unpredictable.

The great Citroëns – the Traction Avant, the 2CV, the DS – were all the work of one man: Citroën's body designer, Flaminio Bertoni. He was a sculptor and a painter, but the crucial event in his life was his move from Italy to Paris in 1932 to work for a Citroën subcontractor. On 27 April he was hired by Andre Citroën himself. During a single night in 1934 Bertoni designed, using a sculptor's tools, the bodywork for the Traction Avant, the car that was Citroën's manifesto. As if to confirm that life in the car design studio was not separate from art in the atelier, in the very same year as he sculpted the

Traction Avant, Bertoni exhibited at the 46eme Exposition des Beaux-Arts at Asnières. Bertoni's next project for Citroën was the TPV ('Toute Petite Voiture'), an exercise in automobile Existenzminimum that was the French equivalent of Dante Giacosa's FIAT 500 and Dr Porsche's Volkswagen. Hitler's war postponed production of the TPV, but in 1949 Bertoni's radical design was launched as the 2CV, which became the beloved *deux chevaux*. Surviving sketches in Bertoni's hand show a Bauhaus purity in the geometry, explicit industrial finishes and a bracing minimalism. In the

The motorcar… broke up family life, or so it seemed, in the Twenties. It separated work and the domicile, as never before. It exploded each city into a dozen suburbs… the motorcar ended the countryside.

Marshall McLuhan, *Understanding Media*, 1964

same year he designed the 2CV, Bertoni exhibited with Giorgio de Chirico at Paris' Salon d'Automne.

In 1938 the Citroën company began work on its greatest ever project, 'VGD' (Voiture de Grand Diffusion). The creative brief was 'Study all the possibilities, including the impossible', which those involved did so very diligently. The result – a magnificent reconciliation of new materials and technology with audacious, sculptural curves and minimalist instrumentation – was the 1955 DS, the car which inspired Barthes. In order that consumers might best appreciate its dramatic form uncompromised by the encumbrance of wheels and tyres, the DS was first shown at the Paris Salon de l'Automobile mounted on a pylon. With a phonic slip, it became the Déesse, and the Goddess became the most remarkable and admired car design of all time.

Although Bertoni was a native Italian, his work as a car designer was wholly in France and entirely French in flavour. The Italian tradition of car design was different from the French and, indeed, from any other national school, being sourced not in manufacturing or technology, but in the old trade of

Opposite: FIAT's Lingotto factory in Turin was designed by engineer Giacomo Matte-Truco and built 1920–23. A concrete structure in full conformity with Futurist art theory, it featured a test track on the roof.

Above: Volkswagen Beetles and Transporters at the Bremen docks, 1966. One designed by an Austrian engineer, the other by a Dutch entrepreneur, each was a symbol of Germany's Wirtschaftswunder.

the *carrozzeria*, or coachbuilder. The greatest of
these is Pininfarina. In 1930–1 Battista or 'Pinin'
Farina established Carrozzeria Pininfarina SpA in
Turin. The achievements of Pininfarina – as it
evolved from artisan metal-bashing to high
automobile art – are a summary of the immense
Italian contribution to the history of car design.

The method of the Pininfarina *carrozzeria*, as
with all others, was to work outside and alongside
the manufacturers, presenting, in the early
days, new bodies on established chassis,
later presenting fully worked-up concept cars
(developed at their own expense) created to lure
manufacturers into lucrative design contracts.

The 1947 Cisitalia was the Pininfarina design that
established a reputation that has endured. Cisitalia
was an idiosyncratic business of no great industrial
significance, but its famous car was celebrated in
its day and has become an acknowledged
masterpiece in the history of industrial design.

In the Fifties Pininfarina became responsible for
a series of cars that defined the age and gave to
sheet steel or aluminium powers of expression
hitherto reserved for marble. The Lancia B20
defined the 'GT', the original idea of a 'Grand
Touring' car with all the attendant baggage of
enlightenment, travel, European trajectories and
personal pleasure. Then in 1951 the Nash Healey
Spider provided styling cues that fed into the
influential California Sports Car Cult. The following
year, the epochal collaboration with Ferrari began.

Above: Battista or 'Pinin'
Farina standing next to his
'Florida II' show car – one
of the most influential
design proposals ever.

Below: The mid-Fifties was
a time of unprecedented
and unreflective wealth.
And nowhere did the
American car flourish better
than California. Magnum
photographer Elliott Erwitt
took this in Hollywood, 1956.

The first car to be called a Ferrari appeared on 12 March 1947. Hitherto, Enzo Ferrari had managed the Alfa Romeo racing team, but his intractable ego and self-worth could not be accommodated in anybody else's corporate structure. So he made his own. In an impoverished Italy of the *ricostruzione* this first Ferrari caused a sensation. It was made with total conviction and no concessions. Between 1947 and 1951, inspired by V-12 Packards that raced at Indianapolis, Ferrari began the development of the glorious 12-cylinder engines which become his trademark. To understand the drama of this, to appreciate Ferrarri's classic bravura, Italy's bestselling car at the time, Dante Giacosa's FIAT Topolino, had a 500cc twin-cylinder engine.

These were the passions which Pininfarina needed to illustrate in its extraordinary series of road cars for Ferrari. Eventually, they became the greatest cars of them all. Enzo Ferrari was interested solely in motor-racing and only made road cars as a concession to business practicalities and because his racing customers demanded them. Ferrari, almost reluctantly, chose to collaborate with Pininfarina. Rarely, if ever, can such condescension have created such ravishing beauty.

Perhaps it was a meeting of minds, or, at least, egos, that made the Farina and Ferrari collaboration so fecund. When it was decided to do business, each was so proud that the one refused to travel to Modena, the other refused to travel to Turin. Instead, they met on neutral ground (it is said)

at Tortona, 70km (44 miles) from Genoa. Pinin drove there in his own Lancia Aurelia B20.

But Pinin continued to work for a range of other clients too, initially in Italy alone, but eventually throughout Europe. His 1954 Lancia Aurelia B24 roadster – a more artistically developed and more conversationally subtle Nash-Healey – brought the formal language he had developed for Ferrari to a larger public. But it was Pininfarina's great rival, Bertone, which was the first *carrozzeria* to design a real mass-market GT. This was Bertone's Alfa Romeo Giulietta, a compact, restrained, but supremely elegant little coupé.

Then in 1955 Pininfarina entered into a contract with Peugeot. It would be inelegant, perhaps, to describe Peugeot (also known as a bicycle manufacturer) as proletarian, but the alliance with Pininfarina extended the reach of Italian design beyond the exclusive Ferrari and the specialists Lancia and Alfa Romeo. Ever since, Peugeot has used Pininfarina as a design consultant.

Influence spread even, yea, unto Longbridge and Cowley, industrial homes of the British Motor Corporation. Since the arrival of Riccardo Burzi in Longbridge from Lancia in Turin in the early Fifties, there had been some covert Italian influence at Austin, but the influence of Pininfarina became explicit when Leonard Lord of BMC signed the maestro. This was not Lord's first encounter with the human exotica of design consultancy: he had also engaged the fabulous Raymond Loewy, but

Reachunder, adjustwasher, screwdown bolt, shove in cotter pin, reachunder, adjustwasher, screwdown bolt, reachunderadjustscrewdownreachunderadjust
John Dos Passos, *U.S.A.:The Big Money*, 1933

the relationship was never consummated with a vehicle. The engagement of Pininfarina led to more fruitful stuff than Loewy's. Soon Pininfarina sketched the Austin A40, the world's first hatchback. And the Morris Oxford shows a fine consanguinity with the contemporary Peugeot 404. This is, depending on your point of view, either evidence of Pininfarina's confident aesthetic or cynical exploitation of credulous manufacturers, selling the same set of drawings twice.

The Pininfarina technique was singular. While in Detroit cars were designed by executive committees responding to marketing plans, features lists and the adjustments required by fixed-cost accountants, in Turin the processes were more artisanal and in direct contact with workshop practices of the Middle Ages. From the most extemporary sketches by the master, a draughtsman would prepared technical drawings. Then a wooden buck would be made. This would

be criticized and adjusted. Sometimes the finished item would be modified, or even destroyed, with a hammer or, more properly, a martello.

The successor to Pininfarina and Bertone is Giorgetto Giugiaro. He was born in 1938 and studied at the Belli Arti in Turin, leaving for FIAT when he was 17. At 21 he joined Nuccio Bertone and in 1965 he became chief executive of the design centre of Ghia. He set up his own firm, ItalDesign, in 1968. While still with Bertone he designed the Alfa Romeo Giulia GT, a car widely considered to be one of the understated classics of all time. ItalDesign worked on the Alfa Romeo Alfasud (1971), on the Volkswagen Golf (1974) and on the FIAT Panda (1980).

The oil crisis of 1973 stimulated a change in Giugiaro's views about design. Having established a particular mode of stylish sporting car he changed to a more practical, more functional one. He even began to practise a form of obsolescence, saying,

I think that cars today are almost the exact equivalent of the great Gothic cathedrals: I mean the supreme creation of an era, conceived with passion by unknown artists.

Roland Barthes, *Mythologies*, 1957

'I contributed to making the long, low, sleek car fashionable, and now it is time to change. I have to eat, you know.' Since the firm has become recognized as *the* leading Italian car consultancy, more and more effort has gone into producing speculative dream cars.

In Britain there was another source of Italian influence, significant not in terms of the mass market, but of the mass-appeal created by aggregates of favourable imagery. The Sean Connery iteration of James Bond drove an Aston-Martin, a car that is apparently the quintessence of Englishness (although Ian Fleming's spy drove a Bentley in literature). However, the beautiful bodies of the DB4 and DB5 were designed and made by Carrozzeria Touring of Milan.

An indigenous native tradition in English car design had three different sources. There was the magnificent country house architecture of John Blatchley in his masterpieces for Bentley and Rolls-

Royce (not, in either case, it must be admitted, wholly without influence from Italy and America, via Pininfarina and Harley Earl: Blatchley's best have fastbacks and fins). Then there was the school of inspired (if financially ruinous) ingenuity and inventiveness which found expression in the exquisite Lotus Elite and austere Mini. Finally, there was the low taste for Americana, perhaps the most influential taste of all.

It was Americana that gave us the Ford Cortina, which, depending on your methodologies, might be considered the most successful of British cars. In terms of technology it was conservative, but in terms of consumer psychology it was consummate: the Cortina delivered a digestible portion of Americana to a population for whom rationing and gas masks were a recent memory. The Cortina's designer was Roy A. Brown, and Brown's career is certain proof of the caprice of consumer behaviour and the almost complete lack

Opposite left: Racing driver Errett Lobban Cord manufactured superlatively sculptural automobiles in very small numbers. This is the Cord 812, 1937. The company did not survive the Second World War.

Opposite right: The great photographer Jacques-Henri Lartigue often used cars as meaningful props in his images of the good life. This is 'Renee en route' (between Paris and Aix-les-Bains), 1931.

Above left: With ponderous handling, great weight and weak brakes, American cars of the Fifties were better suited to the drive-in than to driving. Pierre Belzeaux's photograph captures a culture in thrall to the auto.

Above right: A BMW 328 with special bodywork for the Mille Miglia road race, 1940. In the background is the designer Wilhelm Meyerhuber, who had trained under Harley Earl at General Motors in Detroit.

of rationality in car design. After the flop of the Edsel in 1958, a vanity project whose failure left the Ford management demoralized and embarrassed, Brown was exiled to Ford's Dagenham gulag. In this creative Siberia he drew the epochal Cortina.

The gorgeous and raffish Jaguar E-Type was the near contemporary of the lower-middle-class Cortina. In Jaguar all the elements of British car design came together: a Spitfire-spirit sense of inspired ingenuity; a taste for wood and leather directly attributable to the national preoccupation with visiting country houses; plus a knowing, even sly, commercialism inspired by America. But sex, or a version of it, was the most significant factor in the

E-Type's celebrity. The design is attributed to Jaguar's proprietor, Sir William Lyons, and his aerodynamicist, Malcolm Sayer. The process was intuitive. Significant formal elements were carried over from Jaguar's successful Le Mans sports-racing cars, but clearly the whole was much more than the sum of inherited parts. It seems doubtful that Lyons and Sayer were consciously in pursuit of sexual expressionism, although that is what was achieved. The E-Type's shape, proportions and detail are unambiguously phallic.

Thus the famous and exhibitionist E-Type became the first mass-produced car to be on permanent display in New York's Museum of Modern Art (the first two cars in this shrine of educated taste were the Cisitalia and a Grand Prix Ferrari). It was the Museum of Modern Art that inaugurated the serious study of car design when in 1951 Arthur Drexler curated an exhibition called 'Eight Automobiles'. Some were bespoke craftsmanship, others mass-produced. They were the '30 Mercedes-Benz SS, '37 Cord, '39 Bentley Mark VI, '39 Figoni & Falaschi Talbot, '41 Lincoln Continental, '48 MG TC, '49 Cisitalia and '51 Jeep. Drexler said they were 'rolling sculpture'.

But the acceptance of car design as an important aspect of contemporary culture had its equivalent in a mounting critique of the automobile as a dangerous, polluting instrument of social division. Vance Packard's *The Wastemakers* (1960) mocked consumerism. Ralph Nader's *Unsafe at Any Speed*,

The automobile manufacturers have made, in the past few years, a greater contribution to the art of comfortable seating than chair builders in all preceding history.

Walter Dorwin Teague, 1940

a damagingly critical account of the Chevrolet Corvair's lack of roadworthiness, announced in the early Sixties the beginning of the end of American domination of the global auto industry. Not immediately, but eventually and irrevocably, Nader's account of General Motors' corporate negligence fatally undermined the confidence of one of the world's mightiest manufacturers.

In the year of the Oldsmobile Toronado, General Motors' last great *tour de force*, Ralph Nader made American cars appear both dangerous and ridiculous. Designers had made them look astonishing, but far from keeping slightly in front of consumer taste, Detroit completely failed to anticipate an age of new values. After the Sixties, there was never another great American car.

Now car designers work in a very different cultural environment: industrially, it is all more competitive; socially, less sympathetic; environmentally, much more critical. One hundred years after Ford's 'First Car', technological distinctions between competing vehicles have been to a very substantial degree eroded: while once there were good, bad and indifferent, even dangerous, cars, today the machinery all works well. Legislation requires it. Even if today anyone thought it sane to do a '59 Cadillac, Health and Safety would not allow it. Nor, of course, would the

Opposite: The Jeep was designed to a demanding US Army brief. The result is an enduring design classic: uncompromisingly simple, it cannot be improved. It is shown here during the Detroit race riots of June 1943.

Above: The Pininfarina-designed Cisitalia defined the shape of the post-War Grand Touring car. So pure, simple and structural, it was acquired for the permanent collection of New York's Museum of Modern Art.

environmental lobby. But ferocious competition and stifling legislation have not produced banality in car design – they have encouraged ever greater sophistication. The car buyer is a consumer who understands a marvellously sophisticated language of nuances and gestures.

Consumer choice, at least in the West and Japan, is rarely based wholly on functional, let alone rational, considerations. Instead, consumers choose on the basis of social competition and cultural modelling. Accordingly, the competitive areas in the motor industry are now imagery and symbolism, the absolute substance of art. J. Mays, chief creative officer of Ford, says, 'It's easy to design a part; the difficult thing is to tell a story.' While once 'design' was an industrial option, now it is a commercial imperative.

The car designer's task has evolved in much the same way as the automobile itself. When it is recognized in the market place that the name 'Porsche' is worth more than all the factories, patents and other assets Porsche owns, then understanding and communicating the meaning of that name becomes a paramount business necessity. This has become the contemporary car designer's responsibility.

So you hear as much about DNA in car design studios as in genetics laboratories: every one is concerned to understand how a design transmits meaning across the generations. Everyone is concerned to capture the essence of a brand.

Significantly, the current chief designer at Porsche is English. In Harley Earl's day a Chevrolet was an American responsibility. But international markets and distributed intelligence have made car design international, sometimes surrealistically so. The BMW 5-series launched, to some controversy, in 2003 was designed by an American, Chris Bangle (who used to work for FIAT in Turin). The Rolls-Royce 100EX concept car – a road-going adaptation of an English gentleman's yacht – was designed by Marek Djordevic. And the designer responsible for Skoda's renaissance in the 1990s, a Belgian called Dirk von Braeckl, was promoted to aristocratic Bentley. Here van Braeckl has created a new Continental, using an entirely original visual language which, with great finesse, evokes the country house architecture that John Blatchley, applied to his masterpiece, the 1952 Bentley Continental 'R'. To add another dimension, Bentley is now owned by Volkswagen, manufacturer of the people's car. Clearly, this DNA got lost en route.

Despite their global markets, car designers tend to live in a hermetic world, meeting their peers in airline first-class lounges more often than they meet their customers on the street. Often, their sources of inspiration are bizarre. The Italians were in a quest for a technologically pure *bella figura*. Weight is the enemy and wind resistance the obstacle, according to Felice Bianchi Anderloni and Gaetano Ponzoni. Anderloni was almost certainly the author of the original Ferrari: the 166 Barchetta,

I want that line to have a duflunky, to come across, have a little hook in it, and then do a rashoom or a zong.

Harley Earl, mid 1950s

or little boat. More recently, Pinky Lai, while working in the Porsche studios, cited the Hong Kong Star Ferry, the music of Pat Metheny and trainers as his inspiration. Land Rover's Gerry McGovern has cited women's Lycra-clad bottoms. Others cite guns and Fender Stratocasters. Most designers have a model Ferrari somewhere in their office, although van Braeckl's successor at Skoda, a German called Thomas Ingenlath, has mood boards in his studio encouraging imitation of IKEA's no-nonsense functionalism.

Sources are eclectic, results mixed, but one thing is certain: car design is being forced up an ever tightening helix of creativity. Car design has come to usurp the roles contemporary art has appeared to abandon: the public learns about symbolism, form, about how light falls on objects, how details can articulate meaning from cars… not from the avant-garde.

The car industry requires designers to work to extraordinary disciplines. Someone will know how to remove a few euros of manufacturing costs from a particular moulding. It is not all heroic acts of autonomous creativity: whole careers can be spent achieving little. Circa 1970 at Ford's English design facility at Dunton, Essex, it took 5.7 man

Above: Walker Evans, Joe's Auto Graveyard, 1933. Any car's transit from gleaming desirability to rotting and rusting desuetude is a metaphor of life itself.

months for designers and 9.3 man months for modellers to produce six steering-wheel designs for the Mark III Cortina. It was not even a particularly good steering wheel.

The American corporations have lost their influence. General Motors gave the world the model of a gargantuan corporation with all its parallel divisions, hierarchies, global reach, management science, McKinseyite principles. It stimulated Peter Drucker's management classic *The Concept of the Corporation* (1946) and Alfred Sloan's autobiographical *My Years at General Motors* (1964). Sloan had found a ragbag of provincial engineering firms working on cars and fridges and everything in between and amalgamated them into 'a growth company'.

The great adventure of mass-market car design began when Sloan was brought in to support brand separation. For rather a long time, it was a majestic construct. Now the most impressive sight in the vast General Motors universe is a robot-populated facility in Slovakia, manufacturing cars made by its Korean subsidiary, Kia.

Of course, from the perspective of the twenty-first century it seems very clear that some things are never coming back, the '59 Cadillac being one example. The 1955 Citroën DS and 1963 Ferrari 250 GTO being others. Nor, perhaps, will there ever be a conceptual revolution such as the one that produced the Mini. The great age of car design is over or, at least, assumptions have changed.

Cadillac is bereft, Citroën imports Japanese cars and badges them with André Citroën's idiosyncratic chevrons, Ferrari has become a vulgarian parody of itself, a travesty of the purist principles which inspired its creation. The most significant car of recent years has been the modest smart. An inheritor of the culture of Germany's Kleinwagen, the bubble cars of the Wirtschaftswunder when native engineering genius adapted to regimes of severe restraint, the slow and tiny smart is an ingenious new format that changed the consumer's expectations and enhanced their potential as much as the Mini did 40 years before.

The criteria for the smart included packaging efficiency, fuel economy and low impact on space and resources. So it has very little in common with, say, a Chevrolet Corvette. Except it shares certain basic assumptions about what a car should be: a private, mobile, controlled environment exisiting for the pleasure and convenience of the owner. Hence the Nissan Cube, a car with conventions of beauty left far behind it, but significant because it finally blurs a distinction, a long time eroding, between product design and car styling. It has more in common with an iPod than a Maserati.

Henry Ford's 'faster horses' had their run. Since, a century of glorious inventiveness when 'freedom, style, sex, power, motion, color' and everything else which excites consumers took refuge in the car. Freedom seems a delusion, the rest a selfish indulgence. But magnificent, nonetheless.

Some say the world will end in fire, Some say in ice.
Robert Frost, 'Fire and Ice', 1923

1908

Ford Model T

'Faster horses' was Henry Ford's rationale of the car. He was not the designer of the Model T (that was the work of his friend Childe Harold Willis, assisted by two Hungarian émigrés, Josef Galamb and Eugene Farkas), but it was an expression of his genius. By 1914 it took Ford only 93 minutes to assemble a car. Innovations were not technological nor aesthetic, but social and commercial. The Model T's development was the US system in miniature: as sales rose, prices dropped. The first Model Ts were dark blue, but when Henry Ford discovered black paint dried more quickly, you could have one in any colour so long as it was black. Tough vanadium steel and simple components made it indestructible. By the Twenties, prices had fallen to less than $300. At one point in the car's 19-year life, more pages of the Sears Roebuck catalogue were devoted to Model T spare parts than to men's clothing.

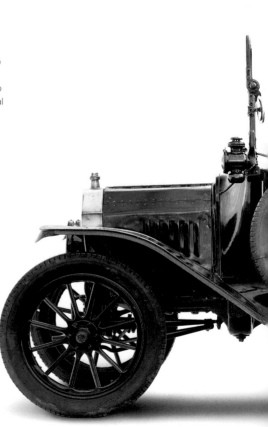

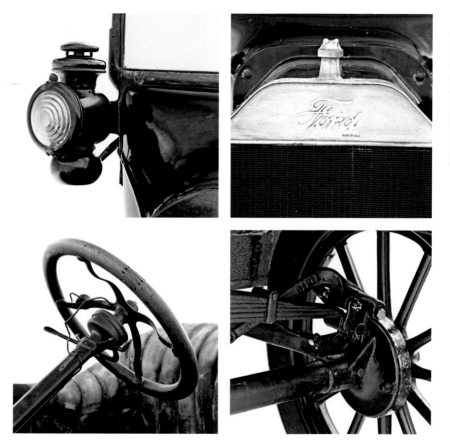

1934

Citroën 11CV Traction Avant

André Citroën was influenced by Ford and by US automated construction techniques. Indeed, with his taste for publicity and his astute understanding of his countrymen's psychology, Citroën could be said to be the French Ford. This car is his Model T, though being French it was more luxurious. From the start, visionary procedures were involved. Safety was an innovation: the first crash test had the car pushed off a cliff. There was front-wheel drive, a rigid body, independent front suspension. The body was drawn by Flaminio Bertoni, an Italian sculptor with connections to the Futurists and Surrealists. The Traction Avant was dramatically lower than its contemporaries: front-wheel drive allowed the placing of the passenger cell between the wheels and closer to the ground. Because of André Citroën's belief that 'dès l'instant qu'une idée est bonne, le prix n'a pas d'importance' costs were high, and led to bankruptcy. Still, Citroën's chief engineer, André Lefebvre, was able to exploit his employer's generous brief. André Citroën built a Champs-Elysées showroom that was more like a museum than a garage. He ran his name in lights up the Eiffel Tower. Under Michelin ownership 800,000 Traction Avants were produced before production ended in 1957.

1934 | CITROËN 11CV TRACTION AVANT

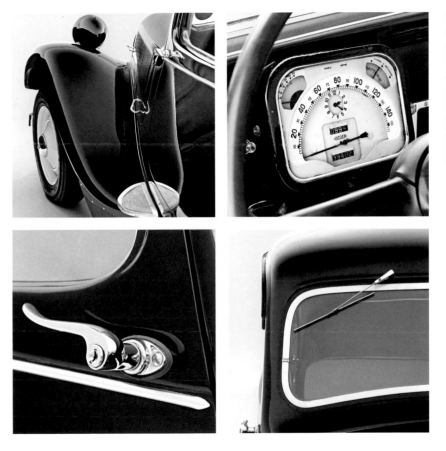

1935

Lincoln Zephyr

Lincoln was Ford's premium brand and the Zephyr was a step up for the consumer from the most expensive Fords. It was a conceit of Henry Ford's son, Edsel. The cable-operated brakes on the Zephyr were *retardataire*, but its light, rigid, monocoque body was radical. The designer was Tom Tjaarda, who had made boat-tailed speedster personal cars for Edsel. While his father was obdurately utilitarian, Edsel had a taste for flash. The Zephyr sloped and tapered unfashionably. With it Tjaarda grasped the slippery semantics of streamlining more successfully than the Chrysler Airflow or the long-forgotten Hupp Aerodynamic by Raymond Loewy. His design was refined by Eugene Turenne 'Bob' Gregorie, hitherto a yacht designer – the Zephyr has a nose like an inverted ship's bow. With 15,000 manufactured in 1936, the Zephyr was an early attempt by a mass-market manufacturer to consumerize luxury and style. Gregorie's design received a US patent and was described by the Museum of Modern Art as the first successful American streamlined car. When production stopped in 1942, Zephyr DNA passed on to the 1941 and '61 Lincoln Continentals.

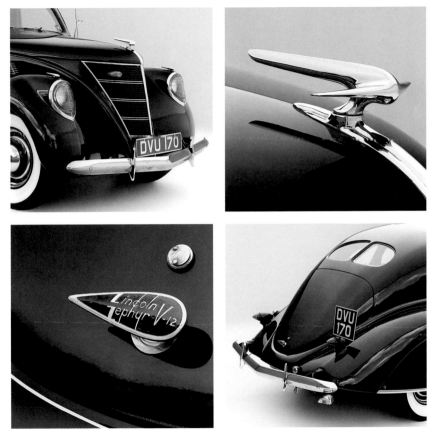

1936

Chrysler Airflow

In this car Carl Breer brought together Art Deco and streamlining. Inspired by the sight of geese flying in a V-formation, and also by the Burlington Zephyr, it became the chosen car of New York mayor Fiorello LaGuardia. Walter Chrysler – a one-time mechanic for Union Pacific Railroad – had a reputation for radical engineering, at least by American standards. The Airflow benefited from pioneering use of a wind tunnel, brought about when an intermediary contacted flight pioneer Orville Wright. It was soon determined that conventional cars of the era were more aerodynamically efficient when travelling backwards. Breer's architecture placed passengers within the wheelbase, to achieve even weight distribution, and the engine was moved forward of the front wheel centre-line. This new geometry allowed a new architecture: influential, wonderful, but commercially ruinous. The Airflow was simplified, then abandoned in 1937, although it was a possible influence on Porsche's Volkswagen. Indisputably, the first Toyota was virtually a copy.

1939

BMW 328 Mille Miglia

Kurt Joachimson's 1936 BMW 328 was the first modern sports car: fast, safe and reliable, with design that expressed that originality. It had faired-in headlights, cutaway doors, a sense of spareness. The essential simplicity is, in fact, a hard-won subtlety. *Autocar*'s road test of 16 July 1937 concluded 'It is difficult to think of this machine in terms that apply to the more ordinary type of car.' The streamlined competition version was drawn by Wilhelm Meyerhuber in BMW's pioneering department of Künstlerische Gestaltung, or artistic development. The shape is both scientifically aerodynamic and lasciviously beautiful; restrained,

yet flamboyantly seductive. No details intrude upon a perfectly conceived whole. A small handful was made by Carrozzeria Touring of Milan. The 328 Mille Miglia, a unique expression of German genius, was a clear influence on the postwar English Jaguar XK120. After the Second World War, the British Frazer-Nash company acquired production rights as part of war reparations. Frazer-Nash-BMWs featured distinctive ventilated steel wheels. The British contribution was having the holes drilled in Middlesex. The British think of themselves as sports car pioneers, but the origin of the modern sports car was German.

1941

Jeep

The predecessor of the Jeep was a stripped-down, weaponized Ford Model T. The US Government made an RFB, or 'Request for Bid', from American Bantam, Ford and Willys-Overland, allowing 49 days for prototypes and 75 days to complete 70 test vehicles. Specification was four-wheel-drive, crew of three, 2.03m (80in) wheelbase, track no more than 1.1m (47in), empty weight of 590kg (1,300lb), 299kg (660lb) payload and a fold-down windscreen. Karl Probst, a freelance designer, submitted a 'Blitz Buggy' for Bantam, but production went to the bigger manufacturers, now working to a more realistic weight limit of 980kg (2,160lb). Delmar B. 'Barney' Roos and a motley crew of army officers also claimed a design role. Officially the Willys-Overland Military Model MB, it is known everywhere as the Jeep. An unimprovably simple diagram of its type, it was consumerized in 1946 into the Jeepster and Station Wagon by designer Brooks Stevens. President Dwight D. Eisenhower said that, along with the C-47 Dakota transport plane and the bulldozer, the Jeep was the most significant piece of Second World War equipment. 'Jeep' became a registered trademark in 1950. The following year a Jeep was shown in the 'Eight Automobiles' exhibition in New York's Museum of Modern Art. Its purity, longevity and usefulness makes a depressing contrast with its successor, the High Mobility Multipurpose Wheeled Vehicle (HumVee), an RFB of 1981.

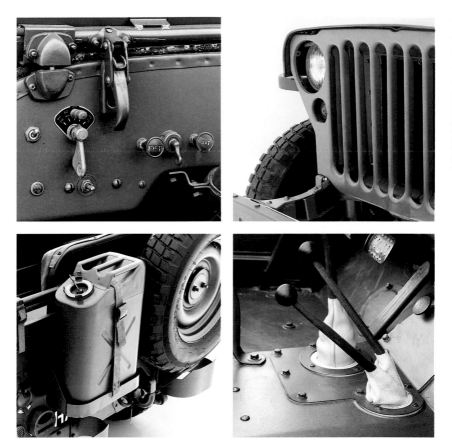

1947

Cisitalia

Piero Dusio founded Consorzio Industriale Sportivo Italia in Turin in 1943. He owned the Beltrame bicycle factory, which had access to the small diameter tubes that made his lightweight cars possible – the famous Cisitalia 202 weighed only 780kg (1,720lb). Dusio hired the best talent to realize his dream of a modern Italian sports car. Engineering studies were by Dante Giacosa, FIAT's visionary engineer. Then Giovanni Savonuzzi was appointed Cisitalia's technical director and he created the beautiful, spare graphic. But it was when Pininfarina devised a closed coupé body for the Cisitalia that a landmark in the history of car design was reached. To Savonuzzi's uncompromisingly functional nose, Pininfarina made sculptural additions. He suggested a pair of aerodynamic stabilizing fins, but these gave way to integrated wings, making the Pininfarina Cisitalia a wonder of formal composition. Despite its different authors, the Cisitalia appears a superb whole. Only 170 were built between 1947 and 1952, but because one of them was exhibited at the New York's Museum of Modern Art's car design exhibition of 1951, it became one of the most influential automobiles of all time.

1948

Cadillac '61

In 1941 Harley Earl arranged a visit to a secret air-force base so his staff could look at the Lockheed P-38 'Lightning', a fighter-bomber with a twin-boom configuration and gorgeous details including erotic scoops and a blister canopy. They were not allowed to take notes, but told to 'mentally recall' every detail. When car production resumed after 1945, Frank Hershey and other GM designers were working on Cadillac's 1949 'Futuramic' series and the P-38 was an inspiration. But there was now a new source of semantic inspiration: the 1946 Lockheed Shooting Star jet. The result was the Cadillac '61, a masterpiece of restrained grandeur. Hershey and his assistant Ned Nickles obeyed

Earl's instruction for the front end to 'look Tiffany'. But aircraft contributed to the continuous, sinuous profile and to those tail fins. Earl's successor as GM design boss, William Mitchell, explained that 'the fins give definition to the rear of the car for the first time.' This was the beginning of the technicolour adventure of the uninhibited, guilt-free kitsch that American car design was to become in the Fifties.

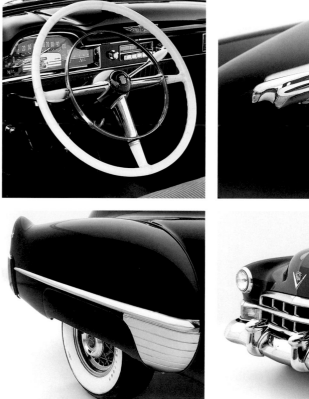

1948

Jaguar XK120

This is the car that made Jaguar's reputation. Perhaps the most perfectly complete expression of the English sports car, it is also a fairly complete expression of English genius in all its flawed, opportunistic, eccentric originality. The gorgeous shape was a sensation when it appeared in the drab, rationed environment of the 1948 London Motor Show. But this most English of cars was clearly influenced by the shape of the BMW 328, especially the Mille Miglia specials. Jaguar's presiding genius, Sir William Lyons, said that the XK120 took just two weeks from concept to a full-sized mock-up. The first cars had handmade aluminium panels over an ash frame, but for production the car had a pressed-steel body with aluminium bonnet and doors. Artistically, it is a satisfying combination of being apparently simple: a clear, unified, flowing form with no fussy effects, but it is also extremely subtle. And, despite the influence of BMW, completely and wholly original. No car body has ever made such voluptuous, but disciplined, use of curves. To build on sensational consumer response, Jaguar did a well-publicized speed trial. On 30 May 1949, with Ron 'Soapy' Sutton at the wheel, a virtually standard XK120 reached a record speed of 213kp/h (132.6mph) on a Belgian autoroute near Jabbeke, close to Ostend. The original price of the XK120 was £998.

1948

Land Rover Series 1

The Land Rover Series 1 is one of the most perfect car designs of all time, but its origins lie in a pleasant muddle and in Welsh puddles. Rover's chief designer, Maurice Wilks, had used a Jeep on his Anglesey farm during the Second World War. Impressed, he decided to better it. The Series I Land Rover used a Willys Jeep chassis and a Rover P3 gearbox. Wilks pioneered recycling with a frugal and ingenious use of military surplus aluminium. Soon Jeep components were being designed out of the Land Rover and it became what German philosophers call a *Ding an sich*, or thing unto itself. By 1950, the stop-gap Land Rover was outselling Rover's conventional cars. It was the beginning of a design language the company is still using. The Series 1 Land Rover is an extraordinary graphic composition, rather like a child's drawing. It is all straight lines, but utterly distinctive. Like the ur-Volkswagen, it is identifiable in silhouette alone. Gerry McGovern, Land Rover's chief designer in 2008, explained that the Series 1 achieved this effect because of its perfect proportions. Overhangs are appropriate to a vehicle of this type and size. Each part is in nice relationship with the whole. Nothing is oversized, or too diminished. The 1948 car was a masterpiece of vernacular chic.

UNO
607

1949

Porsche 356

Chief Designer Karl Rabe began working on the private project that became the Porsche 356 in 1946. It became a reality on 8 June 1948: a two-seater sports car of exceptional lightness and purity of concept. Using standard Volkswagen components, it was designed to achieve ideal performance/weight ratios and to offer minimal resistance to the air. The bonnet of this rear-engined car was not low-slung just for aerodynamic penetration: Porsche theory insisted that the driver should be in emotional contact with the road. The 35hp Number 1 Porsche could reach 135kp/h (84mph). In 1950 Porsche began production of the 'German' 356. Bodies, manufactured by Reutter, were to a design by Erwin Komenda, who had drawn the original Volkswagen. With this car Komenda developed an experimental technical prototype into a mature shape and in so doing created what has become the Porsche signature. Dr Porsche died in January 1951.

American importer Max Hoffman told the younger Ferry Porsche, 'That design is absolutely impossible. You will never sell that car in America.' In August of that year, the 1,000th Porsche was produced. The 356 evolved continuously until the final version was produced in 1965. The absolutely impossible design evolved into the Porsche 911, perhaps the greatest sports car ever made.

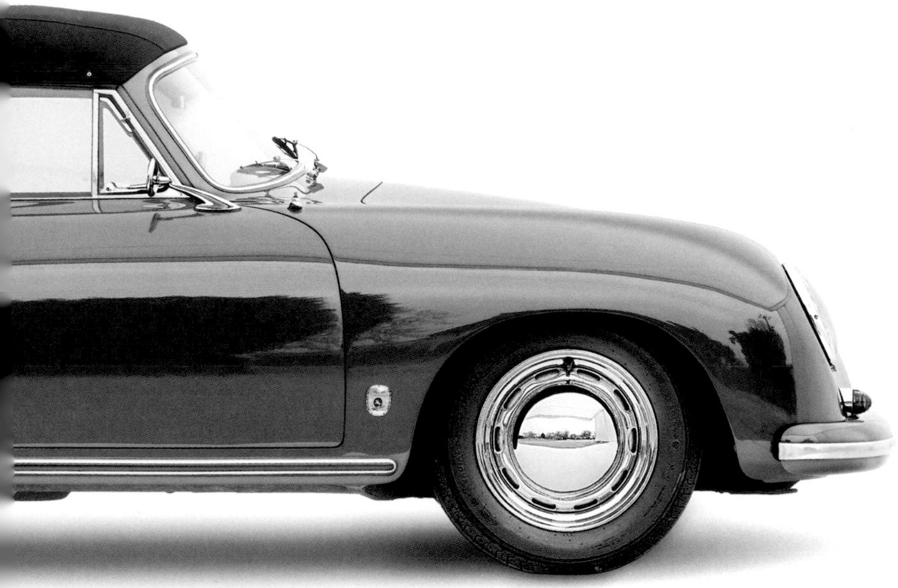

1949

Citroën 2CV

Pierre Boulanger's 'umbrella on wheels' had its origins in Bauhaus principles of truth to materials and geometrical purity, although the brief was in fact more homespun: it was to carry a *paysan* with 50kg (110lb) of agricultural goods at 50kp/h (31mph). The concept was revived after 1945 by Boulanger and engineer André Lefebvre. Launched in 1948 at the Paris Salon, the new Citroën featured aircraft-style tubes under a thin steel carapace. The unique body was designed by Flaminio Bertoni and featured doors and canvas seats that could be removed. Besides the Bauhaus logic, there was a practical rationale for its appearance. The semi-unitary body was inexpensive to make as it used mostly flat stampings, also easy to repair. It was held together by a mere 16 bolts. The roof and the boot lid were canvas. This was both cheap and practical: awkward agricultural objects could be accommodated. Prototypes had a single headlamp. A single indicator unit sufficed. There were no window winders, just hinged flaps. In 1953 the 2CV acquired locks and the cable-pull starter was replaced by an ignition key. A metal boot lid appeared in 1955. Production ended in 1990.

1949

Volkswagen

In 1925 Austro-Hungarian engineer Bela Barenyi presented some proposals for a rear-engined car with a teardrop shape to the Maschinenbauanstalt Wien. The Volkswagen we know today was developed for Hitler by Dr Ferdinand Porsche, after a pronouncement from the Führer at the 1934 Berlin Motor Show demanding a car for the Volk. The Volkswagen contract was signed on 22 June 1934 with a target price of 990 Reichsmarks. In 1936 Hitler decided the project should be sponsored by the Kraft durch Freude movement. Early Volkswagens were thus known as the 'Strength through Joy' car, although it was officially Porsche Typ 60. The Volkswagen, later known as the 'Kaefer' (Beetle) had a body designed by Erwin Kommenda on the aerodynamic principles established by Paul Jaray, although the Chrysler Airflow may also have been an influence. The source of Porsche's own-name sports car concept, the Volkswagen's influence was equalled only by that of the Model T Ford and the Mini. In 1955 the State Patent Office in Mannheim accepted that Bela Beranyi had, in fact, designed the Volkswagen. He accepted compensation of a single Deutsche Mark. Beetle production in Germany lasted from 1941 to 1978; it then shifted to Mexico, where the very last car was produced in July 2003.

1949

Ford

The '49 Ford was a simple car, but a revolutionary one. *Car and Driver* magazine declared it 'the car that saved Ford'. It is almost impossible to attribute it to a single designer because it was the result of a competition between consultants and in-house designers. Anyway, Ford's Ernest Breech said, 'I have a vision. We start from scratch.' This was not quite true, as everybody in the process was influenced by Raymond Loewy's Studebaker. A clay model of the '49 was baked in the oven of Dick Caleal's home in Mishakawa, Indiana. Meanwhile, a Studebaker was bought, disassembled, weighed and labelled. The single greatest influence may have been consultant George Walker. He made

hitherto bulging sides flat and helped to create the simple, elegant, integrated shape. Against this, the spinner nose contrasts nicely. As a result of the '49's success, Walker was appointed Design Director of Ford in 1955. In November 1957 *Time* magazine called him 'The Cellini of Chrome'. In 2001 J. Mays showed a retrofuturist '49 at the North American International Auto Show in Detroit. Mays explained 'by really sharpening and paring down the design, a car was created that looked clean, streamlined, modern… it's so much closer to the cars that followed it and so unlike the cars that immediately preceded it.'

1949

SAAB 92

The vehicle manufactured by SAAB before the 92
was the conceptually radical 21 single-seat fighter.
Designed by a team led by Frid Warnstrom, the 21
first flew in July 1943 and was evidence of genuine
original thinking so, when the aircraft engineers of
Svenska Aeroplan AB found themselves redundant
in 1945 they decided to make a genuinely original
car. Built on aircraft principles with a monocoque
structure, it was given emphatic aerodynamic form.
With the engine placed ahead of the front axle, the
passenger cell and centre of gravity could be low.
The 92's engineer was Gunnar Ljungstrom, who
worked on the 21's wing structure. Ljungstrom
gave the task of body design to Sixten Sason, a
Swedish artist respected as a technical and science
fiction illustrator. Early drawings were gorgeous
gouaches of a terrestrial spaceship occupied by
leggy women. Wheel arches were originally faired
in, but this was found to have practical
disadvantages in the Swedish winter since they
unhelpfully allowed snow and mud to accumulate,
to the detriment of the steering. For production
the design was compromised… but not
very much. The 92 that went into
production was one of the most
advanced small cars ever.

1950

Volkswagen Transporter

The first development of the original Volkswagen car, its van derivative became almost as much of a cult. The Transporter retained the original design's logic and purity, but had a commercial character. Its origins are due to Ben Pon, an entrepreneur from Amersfoort in the Netherlands. Pon met with British occupation forces on 23 April 1947 to discuss his idea. He had seen the Plattenwagen, made by Volkswagen, used to move goods around the Wolfsburg factory. Pon wanted a van that weighed 750kg (1,653lb) and could transport the same weight. Two prototypes, Typ 29, were made and tested but were aerodynamically unsatisfactory. A more curvaceous proposal by Pon was taken up. Although Pon's sketch was intuitive rather than scientific, the bluff-nosed transporter proved to be more aerodynamic than the Beetle. Notable features were the elegant moulding and the unusually prominent VW logo. An amazing focus on cargo space, located precisely between axles, was aided by the symmetrical distribution of engine at one end with driver at the other. The entrepeneur's motorized factory pallet evolved into the California surfer-dude's VW Microbus in the Sixties.

1951

Lancia Aurelia B20 GT

The very first car to be called a GT (or Gran Turismo, in deference to the British tradition of the Grand Tour) was the Lancia Aurelia B20, a coupé version of the 1951 Aurelia B10 saloon. The first cars were manufactured by Carrozzeria Viotti, but Pininfarina soon took over production. Racing successes helped to confirm an image: a two litre B20 came second in the Mille Miglia to a four litre Ferrari. The car was drawn by Mario Boano. Unitary body construction comprised 100 hand-beaten panels, the last time Pininfarina used craft techniques. Although the general arrangement never changed, the B20 went through progressive evolutions up to the Sixth Series; each refined the design and made the car more modern. The First Series B20s were exceptionally austere. The Second Series had a more assertive face with enhanced rear fins. The Third Series appeared in 1953 with wraparound bumpers. The Fourth Series of 1955 is the ultimate B20. There were distinctive push-button door handles and the instrument panel was stylized. Colours were carefully chosen and complementary to cloth trim. Tinted glass was available. The Aurelia B20 GT was the very essence of *bella figura* and defined a lasting automobile type.

1952

Bentley R-Type Continental

This was the fastest four-seater car of its day, also the most elegant and refined. It is the quintessence of English handsomeness, but paradoxically – since it was built for the postwar export drive – none was built for English customers. Its origins were in the Bentley Mark VI, a car designed for economic recovery. The architecture, oddly, owes something to contemporary Americana. The source of the profile, with its distinctive fastback, may even be traced to the ineffably proletarian 1949 Chevrolet Fleetline. The designer was John Blatchley, who learnt his trade at Gurney Nutting coachbuilders. He joined the aero-engine division of Rolls-Royce, where his aerodynamic improvements to the cowling of the Merlin V-12 gave a distinctive performance advantage to Hurricane and Spitfire fighters. In working on the R-Type Continental, Blatchley used the Rolls-Royce wind-tunnel; small refinements arising from testing included angling the radiator back an aesthetically decisive three degrees. What was not attributable to the wind-tunnel was attributable to a combination of good manners and good taste. The R-Type Continental has an aristocratic bearing, but is unostentatious and understated. Surfaces are handled with both great confidence and winning tact.

1953

Studebaker Starlight

Studebaker had a fine reputation, but struggled to compete with the Big Three manufacturers. In the late Thirties management looked to the emergent design profession for help and found the talented, flamboyant, self-mythologisizing Raymond Loewy (who established the first design consultancy in New York in 1927). Loewy opened his own studio within Studebaker's South Bend, Indiana, factory in 1939, working in conditions of mythic secrecy. In 1951, Studebaker's Harold Vance asked him to produce designs for a two-door four-seater coupé. The result was the 1953 Starlight (which has a B-pillar) and its near-identical twin the Starliner (which is pillarless). The ads said it was 'The new American car with the European look'. At 142cm (4ft 8in) it was dramatically low for its day. Loewy's design team included Gordon Buehrig (who designed the celebrated Cord) and Albrecht Goertz (who later designed the BMW 507 and Datsun 240Z), although the autograph of the Starlight/ Starliner belonged to Bob Bourke. But the cars were known as 'the Loewy Coupés'. By a process of critique and recommendation, Loewy exercised his will and the '53 Studebakers were the most complete expression of a designer's concept ever to get into production. Loewy could not distinguish between aesthetic excellence and PR impact, so was delighted when the Starliner appeared on the cover of *Time* magazine for 2 February 1953 with the copyline 'For a sports car era, a long, low whistle-stopper'.

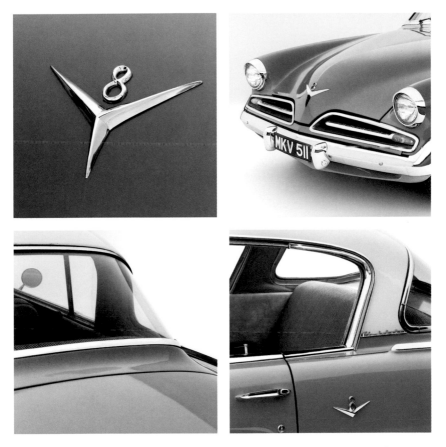

1953

Panhard Dyna

René Panhard had a reputation for conceptual eccentricity, sometimes wilfully so. The Dyna was Panhard's last successful car, which morphed into the Dyna Z in 1954 and was developed into the mature PL17 in 1959. The original design, conceived under the French government's Pons Plan whereby priority was given to economy cars, was all light alloy, but during its life the panels progressively became steel (although the engine remained aluminium). The engine and front-wheel-drive power train was in a modular package and the front end lifted as one. The Dyna offered an unrivalled, indeed unique, combination of interior space, ride comfort and economy, this last from an eccentric flat twin engine of improbably small capacity to propel a large car. Efficient aerodynamics, not wholly uncontaminated by the stylist's bravura gestures, helped to achieve this. As did a low weight, 108kg (238lb) for each of six passengers. Curious details included a knob on the steering column to disconnect the battery. And, long before such rationality became commonplace, all the Dyna's secondary controls (lights, indicators, acoustic warning) were operated by a single lever. This 850cc car could cruise at 145kp/h (90mph) while carrying four passengers. It was a design masterpiece, but a commercial catastrophe. Panhard was bought by Citroën in 1965 and went out of business two years later.

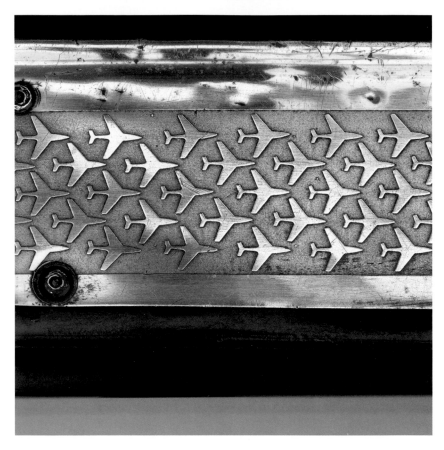

1953

AC Ace

The original AC company was an antique survival of pioneer British vehicle manufacturing. Then, in 1963, a Texan chicken farmer and racing driver called Carroll Shelby (winner of the 1959 Le Mans 24-hour race) had the happy idea of inserting a powerful American Ford '289' V-8 into the hitherto unassuming AC Ace. He named it the Cobra. At the time of its introduction, AC was still using a six-cylinder engine dating back to 1919. The Ford engine had a transformational effect on the Ace's performance, but there were other sorts of alchemy involved as well. The Ace's distinguished aspect (so apparently an English classic) is in fact a blatant copy of Carrozzeria Touring's 1949 body design for Ferrari's Barchetta 166. Other elements in the brew included a tubular chassis by a Cambridge-based Portuguese artisan-designer called John Tojeiro. But, by some mysterious processes, the Cobra became much more than the sum of its parts. Shelby employed some of the graphic language of American hot-rodding to turn a well-mannered English sports car into a swollen phallus of visual aggression. Ride height was lowered and wheel arches enhanced snugly to accommodate dramatic dragster wheels and tyres. Scoops were enlarged, ducts added, chrome details judiciously employed. The Cobra influenced nothing, but was an exquisite example of itself.

1953

Chevrolet Corvette

The 'vette was America's first sports car, a Detroit response to the waves of small, sporty British two-seaters in the years after 1945. When it went on sale in 1953, it was the first production car anywhere to have plastic body panels (although the chassis was resolutely old-regime steel). The first batch of Corvettes was all Polo white with Sportsman red vinyl interiors (the names are revealing of social ambitions). Styling was a shameless display of sexual suggestiveness: the soft red cockpit within a white body may have been unconscious, but was nonetheless dramatically effective. Details were stolen from racing cars and curves were lascivious, but the appearance flattered only to disappoint; with its lazy two-speed Powerglide transmission and unfit 'stovebolt' 3.5-litre six cylinders, known melodramatically as Blue Flame Six, this automobile equivalent of the psychodrama of sex was embarrassingly slow. Not even Harley Earl's evocative jet nozzles could help, and despite a modest $3,250 price, the Corvette was a market failure until in 1955 Chevrolet's small block V8 was fitted and performance was radically enhanced. The Corvette was completely reskinned for 1956, with better colours, more body sculpting, more chrome, but still faithful to Earl's gloriously vulgar original. In 1960 the car was canonized by the *Route 66* television show.

1954

Mercedes-Benz 300SL

No car better demonstrates the consummate German mastery of automobile art and technology than the Mercedes-Benz 300SL. Before the Second World War, Mercedes-Benz had a superb reputation for making limousines, trucks and racing cars. After the war, the company continued Hitler's Silber Pfeilen (Silver Arrows) racing policy, but this time in pursuit of commercial markets, not military conquests. In 1952 Mercedes-Benz won the Le Mans 24-hour race and the US importer Max Hoffmann told the Stuttgart factory he could sell a thousand domesticated racing cars in America, if they could build them. This task fell to designer Friedrich Geiger, with engineers Karl Wilfert and Walter Hacker. Two years after the Le Mans victory,

a house-trained version of the racing car came to market. Signature features included 'gull wing' doors hinged at the roof, made necessary by the longitudinal pontoons, which provided a rigid structure but made conventional doors unfeasible. Details included trapezoidal intakes, a company motif and curious eyebrows over wheel arches. The engine was canted at a 45-degree angle which allowed a dramatically low bonnetline. The whole is an exquisite sculpture of total originality: although the racing car was the starting point, the destination was quite new. Crisp details give a confident, graphic clarity. Long before 'branding' became an issue, the 300SL made emphatic use of Mercedes-Benz' three-pointed star.

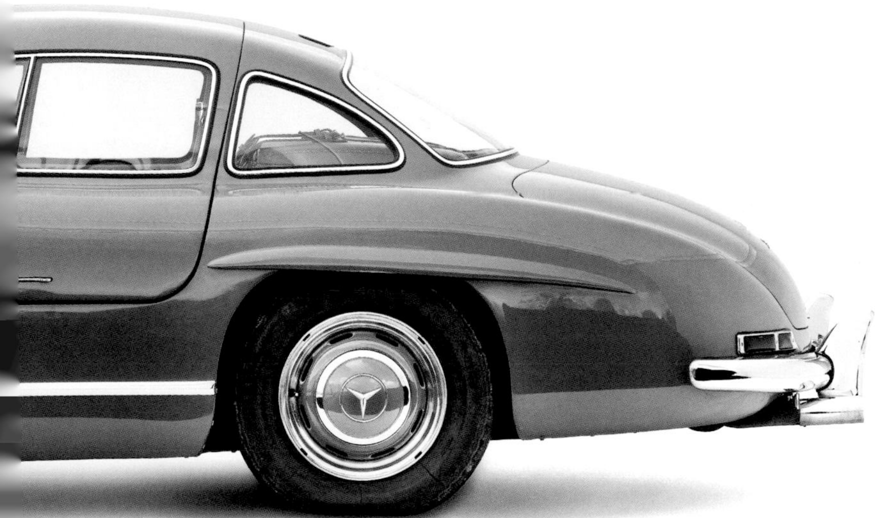

1954

Ford Thunderbird

The Ford Thunderbird is a perfect representative of the age of innocent consumer excess that Tom Wolfe called 'America's Bourbon Louis romp'. The year after its introduction, the United States made more cars than ever before or since. It was conceived as a competitor for Chevrolet's Corvette, but had the advantage of a powerful V-8 engine as opposed to Chevrolet's crude and wheezy six. Original names included Hep-Cat, El Tigre and Detroiter, but when one of the design team, Alan Giberson, remembered seeing a bird struck by lightning with notable explosive effect, he had an inspiration which, vouchsafed in a Dearborn meeting room, became immortal. He was rewarded with a $95 Saks suit. The Thunderbird is total, vulgarian confectionery. It has dummy bonnet scoops. Some versions had 'opera' windows. All versions were seductive: chief designer Franklin Hershey, ex Cadillac '48, a member of the extended Ford family, defined the idea of a 'personal' car, one that was mass-produced but with a bespoke feel. Marilyn Monroe owned a pink one, in a Detroit–Hollywood take on sympathetic magic. Thunderbird demonstrated Ford's understanding of consumer psychology and how meaning can be differentiated by details: a 'Continental' option was chosen by Norma Jean. This included an irrational, but gorgeous, external spare wheel with a hard cover. Other versions had restricted use of chrome. Hershey said that he wanted a banker to feel dignified in a Thunderbird.

1954

Alfa Romeo Giulietta Sprint

This was the response by Carrozzeria Bertone to rival Pininfarina's Lancia B20. The Giulietta was conceived as a moderately priced but elegant addition to Alfa Romeo's range. More mass-market than the aristocratic Lancia, in a sense the Giulietta is the predecessor of the small coupés from the second half of the twentieth century: a two-plus-two, almost effeminately elegant with discreet and modest details within a finely proportioned whole. As a package, it offered the newly emerging Italian middle-class consumer access to a world of sophistication hitherto restricted to a privileged few. As a work of art, it represents Bertone's offer to the consumer of the extravagant aesthetic language he had developed in the BAT (Berlina Aerodinamica Technica) show cars he used to trail his coat in the same year. First versions of the Giulietta Sprint were partially aluminium, and Perspex filled the daylight openings. Popular success meant that this specification was soon value-engineered to steel and glass. There were some special editions, noteworthy most of all for breakthrough nomenclature: the estate version by Carrozzeria Boneschi was called La Weekendina. Production ran to 1962 when it was replaced by the Giulia, drawn by Giorgetto Giugiaro.

1955

Lancia Aurelia B24

Lancia's recent reputation has become mired and confused by years of lacklustre product dictated by opportunistic corporate managers, not inspired by engineers or talented designers. At the same time, a retreat from US and British markets caused by suboptimal consumer response to ruinous problems with rust and reliability has turned it into a ghost brand. But there was a time when 'Lancia' was a synonym for supreme elegance and high performance contained in packages defined by voluptuous, yet dignified, metal. Lancia also made racing cars at least the equal in glory and speed of those by Ferrari and Alfa Romeo. The Aurelia Spider was launched when Lancia was at the peak of its performance. It was specifically designed for the American market, although first shown at Brussels in 1955 (with atrocious fake-wire wheels). Because of American demands, the B24 was rather larger than previous Lancia sports cars. Also with a nod to the US market, Pininfarina clearly construed it as a less expensive Ferrari and provided bodywork obviously inspired by the Ferrari 375 'America'. The bravura (and very American) wraparound windshield of the show car was abandoned for 1956 and flapping Perspex side-screens replaced by wind-up glass. Door apertures became more generous, but a fundamental elegance remained: it is an aristocrat, but with a lascivious air.

1955

MGA

MG stand for Morris Garages and the badge was first seen on an MG 14/40 Mark IV in 1928, an assemblage of humdrum Morris components turned by alchemy and ingenuity into a passable sports car. Up to the mid-Fifties, MG produced two-seaters with an uncompromisingly *retardataire* style. There were no voluptuous curves, but their charm and quintessentially English pragmatism were favoured by US sophisticates. The MGA represented a break with tradition as disconcerting as if the aircraft industry had gone from a string 'n' canvas Sopwith Camel to a streamlined Hawker Hunter without passing through any intervening stages. It arose from Syd Enever's attempts to do an all-enveloping race-car body for the old sit-up-and-beg MG TD. It did not work out, so he started again. The MGA was shockingly radical for MG: its first car with a full-width body. Drawing with tact and restraint, the anonymous draughtsman was sure that he could achieve his effects through understatement and well-judged radii rather than showy flourishes. With intuitive aerodynamics, low aspect and modest details, it was outstandingly modern for its day (even if the components remained antique). The MGA was the last admired product of the famous Oxfordshire company.

1955

FIAT 600

Like the original Zero-A (which became the inimitable Topolino), the 600 was designed by the great FIAT engineer Dante Giacosa. And like the Vespa motor scooter, it was one of the machines that defined Italy's industrial revolution. Once, an Italian would make only one or two journeys in his life, either to emigrate or to do military service. The Seicento gave ordinary Italian people freedom and independence: it was a car for Italians who were all first-time buyers. The 600 was designed to replace the antique Cinquecento Belvedere, or estate car. Giacosa built a life-size plaster model to determine the most efficient space utilization. A part of the cost-cutting brief was to minimize use of sheet metal, so bonnet and boot were atrophied, no metetricious details allowed. 'I progressively eliminated all the edges,' Giacosa wrote. He chipped away at the model, producing an

elemental, but visionary, design: highly original, but somehow utterly familiar. Even the engine was simplified. Giacosa said, 'As soon as I saw even the very slightest chance of simplification, the design was changed.' The 600 was copied in the Soviet Union as the Zaporozhets ZAZ965.

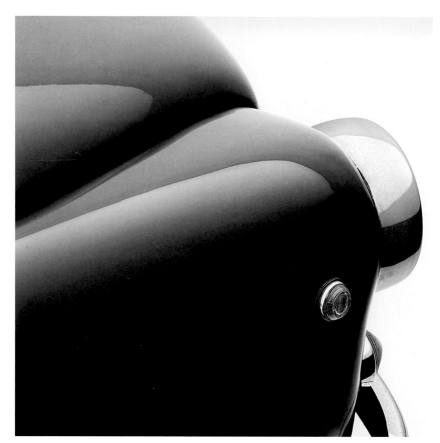

1955

Citroën DS

Perhaps the single greatest automobile design of all time, the DS is an *objet superlatif*, the exaltation of glass. An advanced flat six engine was planned for this car, but budget constraints meant it actually used the same one as the 1934 Traction Avant. But budget was the only constraint: in every other respect, the DS was the most accomplished car ever made. In 1938 Pierre Boulanger started a notebook on the Voiture de Grande Diffusion. He said to his team, 'Study all the possibilities, including the impossible.' Boulanger was killed in 1950 while testing the car, but he had already refined the brief: 'The world's most beautiful, most comfortable and most advanced car, a masterpiece to show the world.' Flaminio Bertoni achieved the greatest work of automobile art. 'Déesse' meant Goddess. First shown without wheels and tyres so as not to compromise the consumers' perception of its pure sculptural form, it was the car that inspired Roland Barthes. High-pressure hydraulics. Self-levelling. Power brakes operated by a button. Automatic clutch. Single-spoke steering wheel. Voluptuously upholstered, astonishing ride. Genuine luxe. Plastic roof with high level indicators, rumoured to have been a late addition when the roof panels distorted to leave an ugly gap. Barthes must have the last word: the DS was the essence of petit-bourgeois advancement.

1955

BMW 507

BMW's department of Künstlerische Gestaltung, a forerunner of contemporary styling departments, was established in Munich in 1938. But it was only in the mid-Fifties that BMW was, once again, able to reestablish an authentic artistic direction of its own. In the Fifties the chief artistic influence on BMW was not so much its German inheritance from the Bauhaus as the twin influences of the American market and Italian style. One of the first cars to point the way to BMW's future was the gorgeous, egregious 507, almost a Bavarian Corvette. It was designed by Dr Albrecht Graf von Goertz, a colourful individual whose gene pool was deeply German and aristocratic, but infiltrated by currents from America. The 507 was, after all, conceived at the same moment that artists in Britain were, through the medium of Pop, celebrating the seductive vulgarity of American culture. Von Goertz had worked in the United States with Raymond Loewy on the Studebaker Starliner and later contributed to the Porsche 911; after 1973, when he became a consultant to Datsun (now Nissan), he was responsible for the 240Z. But BMW's first postwar sports car was von Goertz' masterpiece. The 507 uses explicitly American details and emphatic American form. It is significant as a European designer's projection of American fantasies.

1956

Volvo Amazon 120

Up to the launch of the 120, Volvo cars had been plug ugly. Indeed, so entrenched was the culture of anti-glamour that when designer Jan Wilsgaard presented proposals for the 120 to the company's founders Gustaf Larson and Assar Gabrielsson, the latter commented, 'There is too much of the pin-up about it. It would be better if it was ugly rather than too beautiful.' Critics in 1956 saw both Italian and American influence (Wilsgaard was, coincidentally, born in the States and the first Volvos had been innocent copies of Chevrolets). The 120 was the first beautiful Volvo. It has a coupé-like glasshouse, an elegant profile, a distinctive face and just enough chrome to be interesting. It was the first Volvo available in two-tone paint. Attention was paid to the interior. The instrumentation was

sensibly grouped in front of the driver and there were the first, tentative safety features: padding on the doors and standard seat-belt anchors. Later versions had the first seat designed on ergonomic principles. The lumbar support (adjustable, at first, only with a screwdriver) was made an explicit visual feature. Upholstery was available in all-black, a radical feature at the time. The Amazon established Volvo's enduring brand values.

1956

FIAT Multipla

The FIAT Multipla predicted the phenomenon of the 'people mover', although it had its own Italian predecessors. The first is an extraordinary 1913 Castagna-bodied Alfa Romeo built for Count Ricotti (now in the company museum in Arese); the second, Count Mario Revelli de Beaumont's design studies for a taxi of 1934. Each was well known in Italian design circles. Forward control made the Multipla an exceptional achievement in packaging: a six-seater within an overall length of 3.5m (11½ft), the Multipla's astonishing single-volume unitary body used the components of the successful 600. There were four-, and five-seat and taxi variants available, all offering ingenious variations of the seating arrangements: with all but the front two seats removed, the tiny Multipla had a loading area of more than 1.7sq/m (18sq/ft). Sold to the public in a charming palette of *gelato* colours, the Multipla made its international debut in 1960 when FIAT supplied cars to athletes and officials at the Rome Olympics.

1957

Chevrolet Bel Air

Until the mid-Fifties, US cars were painted in drab colours, then chartreuse, aqua, pink, coral and baby blue became available. The Bel Air was available in most of these and in most conceivable two-tone variations, not all of them sanctioned by good taste. This car, named after an expensive Los Angeles suburb, was a dream car made real. Technologically, it was a vehicle that carried new industry standards, including automatic transmission and power-assisted steering and brakes. Artistically, it represented the ultimate mass-market offer of Harley Earl's concept of styling. Harley Earl's design team comprised Clare MacKichan, Chuck Stebbins, Bob Verkyzer and Carl Renner. The grille was inspired by Ferrari and one commentator spoke of the da Vinci sculpted door handles. All General Motors designers worked to Earl's pervasive brief of going all the way, then backing off some. But the Bel Air team did not back off very much at all.

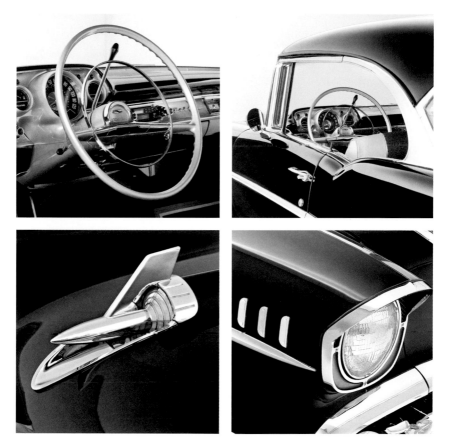

1957

Ford Fairlane 500 Skyliner

Ford had experimented with transparent roofs as early as 1954: access to sunshine was a new variation on the consumer's experience of the automobile. Dealers found they could draw more (male) customers into showrooms with convertibles. Ernest Dichter, President of the Institute for Motivational Research, was commissioned to do some research and discovered that men thought of a convertible as a mistress. It was a lust-filled daydream that lured them into the showroom. Retractable hardtops were the next development. Experiments began at Ford's premium Lincoln Division, but went to market on the mid-range Fairlane. The retractable roof mechanism was ingenious, but complex: a Mahler Fifth of electrical motors, servos, levers and hinges. It added a $350 supplement to the price at a time when the safety-conscious customer could specify seatbelts for $9. Styling features included a clean, full-width chrome grille, twin headlights and graphic side scallop to emphasize two-tone paintwork. Fairlane was the name of Henry Ford's family home in County Cork, Ireland.

1957

Lotus Elite

The car properly known as a Lotus Type 14 is a rare example of an accountant having a beneficial influence in the automobile industry. Peter Kirwan-Taylor arranged financing for Colin Chapman's Lotus Car Company. He drew the first version of the car that is routinely described as one of the most beautiful ever made. It was also one of the most technologically advanced: Chapman was always influenced by aerospace practice and had a fanatical interest in lightness, sometimes at the cost of integrity. Kirwan-Taylor's Elite was the first car ever to have a fully stressed fibreglass monocoque structure. As a result, the Elite weighed 455kg (1,000lb), but the cars suffered problems with flexing and cracking. The resin used to fix the fibreglass also had a propensity to catch fire.

Some of these problems were fixed by Frank Costin, chief aerodynamicist of the de Havilland Aircraft Company. The fibreglass monocoque technology forced an aesthetic simplicity: there were no sharp angles or intrusive perforations. Chapman's motto was 'simplify and add lightness'. Kirwan-Taylor added unusual beauty as well. The Elite is a design from which nothing might beneficially be taken nor to which anything (apart from a rigid backbone) might beneficially be added.

1957

FIAT 500

This car was defined by the Italian townscape: perhaps the smallest viable four-seater ever, it could cope with narrow streets. It was designed for Italian life: a product conceived without cynicism, but with simple passion. This 'nuova' Cinquecento was the successor to Dante Giacosa's original Zero-A or Topolino of 1936. The brief during the period of *ricostruzione*, when Italy had its industrial revolution, was that 'every worker should have a car'. Accordingly, simplicity and economy were decisive. Giacosa was also responsible for the 500. He had a fundamentalist disapproval of excess and spoke of the inspiration he received from the quest for simplicity. He understood the techniques of body construction and designed panels that were cheap to make, but that did not mean they were dull. On the contrary, the quest for economy of means stimulated genius. The 500 has nearly flat glass, but clever pinching and contouring of the body panels makes the whole appear as a generous – if tiny – sculpture, not as a frugal box. Even more so than its predecessor, the 600, the Cinquecento revolutionized Italian social life. It won a Compasso d'Oro in 1959 and remained in production until 1975. In 2007 FIAT revived the Cinquecento with a design by Roberto Gioleti, which pays frank homage to Giacosa's original.

1958

Nash Metropolitan

The Nash Metropolitan (from Birmingham) first greeted the public as the experimental Nash-Kelvinator NX1 on 5 January 1950. Unusual for an American car of its day, the NX1 attempted technological economy within an artistically unusual package. The prototype was shown in a deep shade of maroon, itself an unusual choice. The design of the actual body was even more unusual. It had integrated front bumpers and the entire front-body assembly opened as a single unit. There was no exterior boot lid and access to the luggage space was via the interior. These economies meant an astonishingly low weight of

612kg (1,350lb). The style was wholly original with neither predecessor nor, it must be admitted, followers. Originally powered by a FIAT engine, in March 1954 the NX1 crossed the Atlantic to become the Austin Metropolitan, after designer Bill Fajole had been given a Lucas headlamp bezel and asked to adapt the NX1 architecture to this British component (which he described as 'lousy'). While conceived as an offer of European discipline in the US market, in Britain the little Nash (as it became known) was wistfully interpreted as a miniature of Americana: a moderne hardtop with two-tone vinyl upholstery and ice-cream palette for exterior paint.

1959

Jaguar Mark II

The Mark II was the evolution of Jaguar's 2.4 litre Mark I, launched in September 1955 just a few months after a Jaguar D-Type won the 24-hour Le Mans race. The compact saloon had unitary monocoque construction. A comparison with its exact contemporary, the Citroën DS, is instructive. The Jaguar's language depends on prominent, generously curved front wings that take a line rearwards into an elegantly sloping torpedo tail. For the 1960 Model Year, Jaguar introduced this car: the Mark II compact had a bigger 3.8 litre engine, but the aesthetics had been brightened and tightened too. Window area had grown, pillars were thinner, ovoid grille more egregious, chrome highlights tipping the car towards the raffish personality it later defined among its customers. Compact Jaguars were extremely successful in motor racing and rallying. The Mark II defined the concept of the English sports saloon. Best seen in British racing green with red leather upholstery and chrome wire wheels, it lasted until 1969, by which time it was an elegiac memento of a lost England.

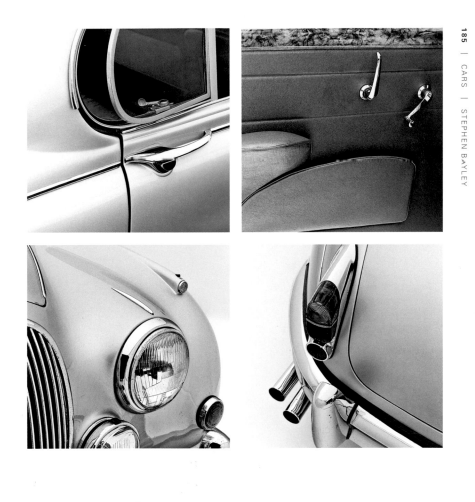

1959

Volvo P1800

The P1800 was Volvo's first sports car, designed as an image-builder for the company. The Ghia and Frua *carrozzerie* made early submissions for a two-seat coupé based on Amazon mechanicals, but management chose a car designed in-house by Pelle Petterson (who later devoted himself to naval architecture and the Americas Cup). Photos of the 1959 prototype showed a car very close to the one that went into production two years later. The P1800 has dramatic proportions with an enormous bonnet (way too commodious for the humble four-cylinder engine it houses, but it is there to suggest ample power) and a small, low glasshouse placed well back. Surfaces are complex with curious changes of radius and direction: the beltline turns

from a roll to a razor edge as it moves rearwards. Critics thought the chrome emphasis on the flanks an error of taste, although it proved distinctive. The front fenders and lights have a striking prognathous look; the grille is expressive. Inside, it is an exercise in controlled Americana: prominent instrument bezels, emphatic use of pleats and plastic. An opening rear window had been an intention, but this was realized only when the Coggiola company of Turin showed a P1800 'ES' prototype in 1968, a coupé with a load deck – the first car in this format.

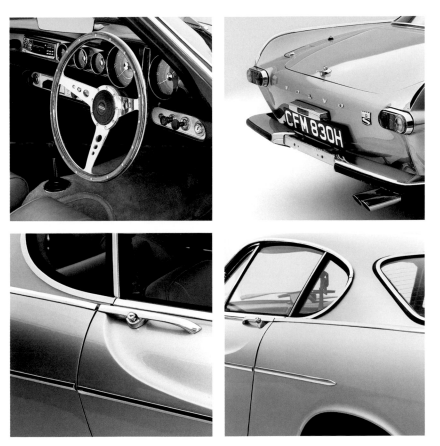

1959

Chevrolet Corvair

Chevrolet engineers began experimenting with a rear-engined design code-named Cadet just after 1945, but a market for conventional cars was no incentive to experiment. But by the later Fifties, the success of the Beetle had forced a revision. The Corvair may have been influenced by Porsche's Volkswagen in terms of general arrangement. The engine itself may have been influenced by the classic Lycoming aircraft engine. But, while radical, the Corvair had neither Porsche's dynamic integrity nor aerospace's quintessential lightness. Indeed, the value-engineered and underspecified swing-axle rear suspension together with an overweight engine contributed to the series of accidents that made the Corvair the subject of Ralph Nader's consumerist polemic, *Unsafe at Any Speed* (1965).

But, safety apart, it was positively outstanding. The 900 Monza (originally a special edition created by designer Bill Mitchell for his daughter) was a sporty compact with pleated bucket seats. Meanwhile, the big glasshouse and emphatic beltline of Ned Nickles were a profound influence on Sixties BMWs. Lights were, influentially, treated as jewellery. In May 1965 Dr Seymour Charles, founder of Physicians for Automotive Safety demanded a total recall of all Corvairs.

1959

Austin A40

The civilization that brought Britain the Kenwood Chef and the first supermarkets also produced the Austin A40. It was Leonard Lord of the old British Motor Corporation who inspired two completely different products, each launched in 1959. The first was the radical Morris Mini Minor (later the 'Mini'), the second was the more technologically conservative Austin A40. It was based on the quaint Austin A35 (whose bulbous body was designed by a Birmingham-based Italian called Riccardo Burzi, inspired by a Lancia original). But Lord hired Pininfarina to create an exceptionally modern shape for the A40. With its fine proportions, razor-edged styling and unique hatchback (in the Countryman version), it suddenly graduated from being merely utilitarian to desirable. The A40 hinted at a notion that did not exist in 1959: lifestyle. Pininfarina had begun to make English contacts in 1957 when he had been voted a Royal Designer for Industry. The year before, he had begun his ambitious collaboration with Peugeot, the first manufacturer to bring his work to the mass market.

1959

Mini

The Mini is one of a handful of great, undisputed car designs of all time. It is an example of the synoptic genius of Alec Issigonis, a martinet, intolerant of authority and hierarchy. Issigionis' design was stimulated by the 1956 fuel crisis caused by the Suez invasion, but had to conform to the stern brief he set himself. Issigonis had a concept of a car only 3m (10ft) long, but with 80 per cent of its length devoted to passengers. To achieve this, he turned the engine sideways. The 24cm (10in) wheels limited intrusion into the passenger cell and gave the car a unique stance. The gearbox was expensively, but ingeniously, placed within the engine's crankcase. There were sliding windows and plastic string door pulls. The minuscule Mini had astonishing internal storage for people and things. However, the uncompromising Issigonis believed it was safer for the driver to be uncomfortable so he deliberately chose an awkward driving position. The Mini's distinctive body was a scaled-down version of the XC9001, an abortive project of 1956. Issigonis eschewed styling but achieved unconscious chic. The Mini was impossible for a snobbish British consumer to categorize and thus became the first small car to be perceived as classless.

1959

Cadillac Eldorado Biarritz

This is Harley Earl, chief wizard in the den of kitsch that was mid-century Detroit, at his delirious best: the ultimate in auto baroque. From the restrained grandiosity of the '48 Cadillac, Harley Earl drove the company through an ever-tightening helix of inventiveness. Rapidly evolving Cadillac form was the pink and chrome illustration of planned obsolescence (although they preferred to call it the 'dynamic economy'). By the mid-Fifties, Cadillac bumpers had outrageous projecting cones, known as 'Dagmars' after the one-name star of the late-night television series *Broadway Open House*; Dagmar was known for her provocative bosom. Cadillac advertisements spoke of 'inherent dignity and grace and beauty'. That cliff of chrome was meant to transmit solidity and endurance. The

interior offered 'lasting luxury and beauty'. The '59 Cadillac was chosen by *Life* magazine as the cover shot for an issue devoted to the century of the automobile. In 1959 such a choice made sense. The '59 Cadillacs pioneered cruise control, almost a metaphor of the garish, somnolent arrogance which defines the car and, perhaps, its customers. So emphatically American, the nomenclature betrayed incongruous yearnings for an exotic Europe so conceptually distant from the Mid-West. Biarritz was the convertible; Seville, the hardtop.

1961

Lincoln Continental

The '61 Lincoln, launched the year Ernest Hemingway shot himself, the same year that 'Runaround Sue' was a hit, was the first US car to escape the Golden Age of Gawp, the artistic language of 'Detroit Machiavellismus'. The Lincoln is a complete original, but shares significant morphological details with the pillbox hat of one of its most famous passengers, Jackie Kennedy. (The hat was a design by Oleg Cassini, whose brother coined the expression 'Jet Set'.) Considered as a formal composition, the Lincoln disguises its vast bulk with exquisite proportions and bravely undecorated surfaces. Like a Donald Judd sculpture, metal is allowed to express itself in bold horizontals. The brightwork on the fenderline emphasizes plastic confidence rather than exaggerated glitz. The massive grille is chrome, but well-mannered. This is the car that pioneered curved sideglass, giving it dramatic tumblehome. Its designers Eugene Bordinat, Don De La Rossa, Elwood P. Engle, Gayle L. Halderman, John Najjar, Robert M. Thomson and George Walker won the US Industrial Design Institute Award for Overall Excellence. The dark blue example John Kennedy used was painted funereal black after the infamous events on Dallas' Deeley Plaza.

1961

Jaguar E-Type

This was the most exciting and beautiful car ever designed for mass-production. An evolution of the D-Type racer and E2A prototype, the design drew on Jaguar's backlist of glorious shapes, most particularly Malcolm Sayer's D-Type. This was a successful racing car designed by men in brown coats, a brilliant demonstration of the art and craft of penetration. A later Jaguar designer, Geoff Lawson, called it 'the optimum expression of steel'. Sayer and Lyons may have been influenced by Alfa Romeo's Disco Volante, but they achieved a unique synthesis. Elegant and aggressive, its phallic proportions amaze, but are moderated by the sober composition. Details have a feminine delicacy, although the faired-in glass headlamp lenses lasted only two years before they were legislated out of existence. The first production car in New York's Museum of Modern Art, it makes contemporary sculpture look ham-fisted. It is proof that cars can be sublime works of art.

1961

BMW 1500

Among the Neue Klasse series of 1961 were BMW's first truly modern cars, produced by a design team led by Wilhelm Hofmeister. There is a purity to the form of the 1500 and a precision in its details, a clarity in its structure, an implied hierarchy in the accumulation of meaningful details plus the suggestion of a strict, controlling intelligence that is, in its way, a complete expression of the prewar Bauhaus ideal. As Walter Gropius, the Bauhaus' founding director said, 'We aimed at realizing standards of excellence, not creating transient novelties.' Novelties included in the new 1500 established a template for BMW design over the next 40 years. Hofmeister had been educated at the Hamburg Wagenbauschule and brought an engineer's disciplines to the art of car design, first as Head of Body Engineering, then as Chief Engineer. The 1500 has the BMW signature details which he authored: the prominent beltline, the big glasshouse and the reverse bend in the C-pillar – known as the Hofmeister-knick – which survived even Chris Bangle's radical assault on BMW design in the twenty-first century. A BMW 1500 painted in bone with tobacco leathertex upholstery, supremely satisfying to the eye, is the perfect demonstration of Ludwig Mies van der Rohe's dictum: 'The Bauhaus was not an institution – it was an idea.' The Bauhaus was a Neue Klasse BMW.

1961

NSU Prinz

The 1961 Prinz was a subcompact, rear-engined four-seater, originally with a two-cylinder motor. It represents a coming together of several significant influences. A background in the world of advanced German motorbikes gave NSU sophisticated technology, but it was the sighting of the Chevrolet Corvair by an NSU board member on an American trip that gave the Prinz its unique appearance. Like the Corvair, the Prinz had a distinctive flying-wedge roof with lip, a big glasshouse and a prominent beltline that radically separated the upper and lower portions of the car. But, unlike the Corvair, the Prinz had this in a package of *Kleinwagen* proportions: designed by Claus Luthe, it was a mere 3.43m (11 ft 3in) long, a jewel. Lightweight, compact high-performance engines made successive versions of the Prinz a pioneer of the compact sports saloon category which BMW later made its own. But when Volkswagen took over NSU in 1969 it was phased out, since management thought its rear-engined format competed with the Beetle (which remained in production in Europe until 1978).

1961

Alfa Romeo Giulia

Alfa Romeo's Museo Storico in Arese near Milan has an example of the Tipo 103, an experimental small car that never went into production. But it carries most of the styling cues that made the Giulia one of Italy's most handsome modern cars. It is overtly '*tre volumi*' or three boxes: nose, cabin, boot. They said that it was 'designed by the wind', but it was actually designed along the aerodynamic precepts established by Dr Wunibald Kamm, the German wind-tunnel experimenter. The Giulia has a small frontal area, a curvaceous screen, body fluting that channels otherwise disruptive air, a tiny spoiler integrated into the trailing edge of the roof and a signature cut-off tail (or 'Kammheck'). To this distinctive general arrangement was

added Alfa Romeo's handsome grille with attendant brightwork and *modernismo* twin headlights, together with an airy glasshouse. Although it gives an impression of being boxy, on further inspection the Giulia reveals itself to be a very subtle expression of the car designer's art. In fact, most edges are carefully radiused.

1961

Renault 4

The first advertisements for the R4 (known affectionately as '*La Quatrelle*') showed the car as a wire shopping basket with the caption 'Elle supermarche bien', confirming its utilitarian nature. Panels were flat and undecorated, the interior spartan, canvas seats on tubular frames could be removed. The R4 abandoned the rear-engined format of its predecessor (which had, curiously, been designed by Dr Porsche while in a French prison). Instead, its brilliant packaging was achieved by a compact engine sitting over the front axle. The first model sold in France was the R3, or *trois chevaux*: a deliberate suggestion that it was the successor to Citroën's ineffable two-horse-powered basket. Doggedly utilitarian, but charming, too, the R4 is an example of French design at its best: the unforced chic of the vernacular, as *typique* as a Duralex glass or a Bic pen. In this it was a successor to the notable range of French small cars that had been inspired by the postwar austerity legislation known as the Pons Plan. While the British Austin A40 in fact pioneered the hatchback format, the R4 (which sold 200,000 in its first year of production) made it popular. The *Quatrelle* had an agricultural aspect, but was in its way a fine shape. As the Russian journalist Iya Ehrenburg said, the French 'would put up with a feeble engine, but not ugly proportions'.

1962

Lancia Flavia Zagato

The *carrozzeria* of Ugo Zagato was founded in the Milanese suburb of Terrazzano di Rho in 1919. Zagato built the bodywork of the magnificent Alfa-Romeo 158 and 159 which won the World Championship in the very first years of Formula One in 1950 and 1951. In road cars of the Fifties, Zagato began to use Plexiglass, a malleable material allowing the creation of sculpturally ambitious curves. Lancia introduced the polite, elegant Flavia saloon in 1960, a car whose expensive technical refinement contributed to the company's eventual bankruptcy. Zagato created a special-bodied Flavia known as the Sport in late 1962. It was designed by Ercole Spada, Zagato's in-house stylist who had joined the firm in 1960,

aged 21. Spada had a wilful genius for emphatic, sometimes even uncomfortable, form. This is the most eccentric of Zagato's designs, developing the 'Panoramico Zagato' motif of the rear glass running into the roofline which was seen on show cars in the late Fifties. This rear-side glazing exploits roof space and gives passengers a unique panoramic and climatic experience: other manufacturers had experimented with similar devices, but only Lancia had the audacity to engineer opening windows.

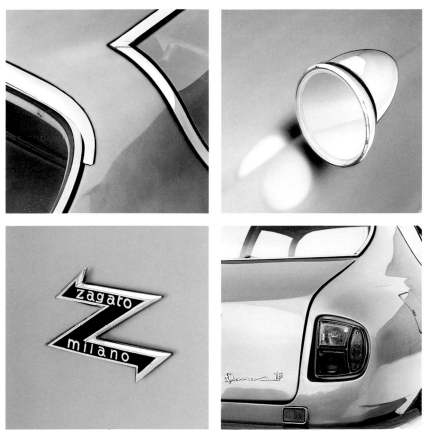

1963

Ford Cortina

The Ford Cortina has some claim to be the most successful British car of all, if not the most technologically adventurous or influential. It began as the Cardinal, a Detroit project for a subcompact which Lee Iacocca killed when he became the head of the Ford Division of FoMoCo in 1960. The Cortina was named after the Dolomites resort Cortina d'Ampezzo, home of the 1956 Winter Olympics. Previous cars in the same category had been named after tweedy and woolly university towns Oxford and Cambridge. Cortina was, on the other hand, for the plastics and nylon generation. There were other international influences, too. Designer Roy A. Brown had worked in Detroit for George Walker on the calamitous Ford Edsel.

As a punishment, he was sent to the Siberia of Ford's English plant at Dagenham in Essex. Out of this humiliation there came the much-loved Cortina. Its secret, at a time when competitors were still offering cars whose interiors were modelled on country houses, was to offer a digestible dose of Americana to a generation just getting used to 77 Sunset Strip on the black-and-white telly. There was chrome, but not too much.

1963

Porsche 911

This is the successor to the first Porsche, the 356. The body evolved from drawings made in the Fifties by Ferdinand-Alexander Porsche, who later left the family firm to establish the independent Porsche Design. At the time, Butzi, as he was known to the family, was driving a Pontiac station wagon. 'In his day,' Butzi said of his grandfather, Dr Porsche, 'a designer did everything.' But by the time of the 911, a division of labour had had its effect, and Butzi Porsche acknowledged the infiltration of perfidious styling into the Holy Rites of engineering purity. 'Styling doesn't exist to provide new faces. It must strive for what is truly good.' The design is clearly based on Erwin Komenda's original Volkswagen and his Porsche 356. On 9 June 1960 the Porsche management sanctioned production of a six-cylinder engine for the 901. While derived from the aesthetic of the 356, Butzi Porsche's design optimized the shape, making it longer and – at his father Ferry Porsche's insistence – capable of carrying a bag of golf clubs. While officially it was the Porsche Typ 901, Peugeot made legal claim to all three-digit denominations with a zero in the middle, so it became the 911.

1963

Buick Riviera

This was one of the ultimate 'personal' cars, the last gasp of American consumerism during Detroit's decadent Hellenistic period. The body was drawn in the General Motors Tech Center in Warren, Michigan by Ned Nickles. The Riviera was the first great GM car after Harley Earl's retirement on 30 November 1959. The Riviera name had first appeared on a Buick Roadmaster in 1949, but Nickles' boss Bill Mitchell claimed to have been inspired by a Rolls-Royce seen in London one foggy night. The Riviera was conceived as a fully developed consumerized treat: so much so that the McCann Erickson ad agency did the design presentation to GM management. In the absence of any compellingly individual engineering philosophy, Buick depended to a special degree on the sort of desires stimulated by design and advertising. Often these were of an only faintly disguised erotic nature. In the Fifties Buick ran shameless advertisements with the copyline 'It makes you feel the man you are.' In the book *The Hidden Persuaders* (1957) Vance Packard revealed more of the occult sexual motivation. Buy a car that 'puts 12,000 pounds of thrust behind every engine stroke' he wrote. Or buy a car that's 'hot, handsome, a honey to handle'. That, for a very brief moment, was the gorgeously sculpted '63 Riviera.

1963

Rover P6

The Rover P6 is one of the greatest English saloon cars. While its predecessor, the stately P5, was favoured by government officials and royalty, the P6 was directed at another market: the emergent executive class. Sold as the 2000, it was designed by David Bache. The younger Bache joined Austin in Birmingham in 1948 at the age of 23. Here he came under the influence of Italian designer Riccardo Burzi. Bache then joined Rover in 1954, participating in the P5 project. But the 2000 was a completely radical car, the most modern large car ever made in England. Originally designed to be powered by Rover's darling gas turbine engine, more conservative engines were tactfully employed. Like the Citroën DS, the 2000 had unstressed metal panels attached to a vast unitary frame. And like the DS, its shape was totally original, with neither precedent nor successor. Unlike the DS, however, its design featured radical innovations in safety and ergonomics. Seat belts were standard for the sculpted front and rear bucket seats. Minor controls were logically arranged and switches were designed to break cleanly in an impact. An ingenious extension of the front headlamp lens refracted light, enabling drivers to pinpoint the nose accurately after dark.

1963

Mercedes-Benz SL

Paul Bracq was born in Bordeaux in 1933, trained in Paris' art school system and worked for industrial designer Philippe Charbonneaux, who specialized in car and truck design. In 1957 he joined the design studios of Mercedes-Benz in Stuttgart, where one of his first projects was to work on the Model W113, launched as the 230SL in 1963. In Mercedes-Benz' language 'SL' stands for 'Super Leicht'. With an empty weight of 1,295kg (1.2 tonne), the SL was not emaciated, but Bracq created a design language whose unfussy, elegant linearity seemed to express concepts of lightness and athleticism, though not of insubstantiality, something which might have been ruinous to Mercedes-Benz' reputation for solidity. Viewed in side elevation, the SL is an arrangement of parallel lines. Viewed in frontal elevation, Bracq has made emphatic use of the Mercedes-Benz star in a dramatically spare composition of air, metal and glass. The signature 'pagoda' roof dips towards the middle and adds distinctiveness to distinction, but it was, in fact, a safety feature. The design of the SL betrays much influence from Bela Barenyi, Mercedes-Benz' Hungarian safety guru who filed 2,500 patents during his working life. One of them was in 1956 for the roof design, a feature that enhanced rigidity and offered better passenger protection in the event of a vehicle inversion.

1963

Chevrolet Corvette

The original Chevrolet Corvette appeared in 1953, an American attempt to come to terms with the English and Italian imports flooding the market after the creation of the Californian sports car cult of the late Forties. Harley Earl's original was produced in a run of only 300, but it was the first mass-produced car to use a fibreglass body. In everything except style the Corvette was a compromise (its lazy six-cylinder engine could scarcely turn its two-speed Powerglide transmission). But the style – which pioneered the wraparound windscreen in a production car – was sensational. Prototypes of its replacement began to appear in 1959; like the original, they were previewed in Motorama road shows. Innovations in the coupé in 1963 included hidden headlights, doors cut deeply into the roof,

an aggressive profile and a distinctive split rear window. The dramatic whole was enhanced by glorious kitsch details including fake air vents and bogus knock-off wheels. Design responsibility had now passed from Earl to Bill Mitchell, who trained at the Barron Collier ad agency, joining GM Art and Color in 1935. Mitchell explained his creative philosophy like this: 'Pick up a billiard ball and it's boring. But pick up a baseball with all that texture and stitching and you play with it for hours.'

1963

Panhard 24CT

The Panhard 24CT is an elegiac car: the very last serious automobile produced by an independent French manufacturer. And, in this case, the manufacturer was the successor to Panhard et Levassor, one of the industry pioneers. A year after the 24CT went on sale in 1964, Panhard was sold to Citroën. The 24CT was light, elegant, conceived with intelligent economy, but executed with a stylish *joie de vivre* and an intensely French suggestion that luxury can be enjoyed on any budget. Its mechanical layout followed well-established Panhard principles. There was a small, flat twin engine, but it was nonetheless a large car. An efficient aerodynamic body was an aid to curiously high performance. The 24CT was designed in-house and betrays many of the quirky idiosyncrasies that characterize French architecture and furniture design of the Sixties. There is an emphasis on horizontals and sometimes demanding angles, yet the sense of sculptural form is unambiguous. The general arrangements can be traced back to the Panhard Dyna, but are here stretched, stylized, modernized.

1963

Ferrari 250 GTO

This is the ultimate expression of the Ferrari idea. Enzo Ferrari said, 'I have never travelled anywhere as a tourist and have never had a holiday… for me the best holiday is going down to the factory.' The 250 GTO, an evolution of the 1959 250 GT, appeared at a press conference in February 1962. It was empirical aerodynamics, a version of its predecessor the 250 GT with a short wheel base, but optimized for racing. They modelled it in plaster of Paris over cloth. It was the evolution of a singular identity. Then Giotto Bizzarini went to the University of Pisa wind-tunnel. As a result, the car had a long, low snout, small radiator aperture, three evocative aerospace-style ducts, a rising tail, a fastback and an integrated spoiler. The 'passenger' had to contest space with the oil tank. Sergio Scaglietti was an inspired interpreter of Pininfarina's drawings, although in the case of this car it appears he used only the Pininfarina 'idea' of a Ferrari as a starting point. Enzo Ferrari himself was only concerned with racing – he said that he sold cars on Monday to pay his mechanics for working on a Sunday. It was Pininfarina's achievement to create a language that expressed this monomaniac devotion. Thirty-nine 'reproductions' of the original idea were built between 1962 and 1964, each one subtly different, the product of Sergio Scaglietti's hammer.

1964

Ford Mustang

The first drawings of the Mustang were made by John Najjar in January–February 1962, a response to a brief from Lee Iacocca formulated, the colourful myth has it, by Ford men and J. Walter Thompson men over steak and beer at Dearborn's Fairlane Inn. Target markets were defined as economy buyers, young performance buyers and affluent, middle-aged buyers. In the end, everyone bought it. Many designers can claim authorship of the epochal Mustang, although perhaps Dave Ash and Joe Oros have ultimate claim. Eighteen clay models were made. Long hood, short deck, muscular aspect: the details were a catalogue of a nation's obsessions. The Mustang sold 518,000 in its first year. A Fastback version came in 1965. It was the ultimate consumer product: a brilliant slice of Americana, the Detroit equivalent of a Morris 1100. It was a masterpiece of simulation, with racing stripes and accent paints. Recite the options and it sounds like e. e. cummings. But it flattered to deceive, and had atrocious driving dynamics: the manual required the tyres to be inflated to 40psi if 'precision driving' was planned.

1964

Pontiac GTO

Designer Bill Porter was influenced by a number of sources. First, Harley Earl's 'highlight rule'. Porter's dramatic profile makes the highlight run the entire length of this 2.92m (9ft 7in) wheelbase car. But Porter also cited de Kooning, Brancusi, Frederick Kiesler and Charles Eames. His design method was based on 'surface development' disciplines of coachbuilding. He did four-view orthographic drawings, then he did sections and then the sections were turned into a 1:5 model by the application of clay. Real and apparent proportions played an important part in perceptions of the Pontiac, not least to alter consumers' perceptions of a brand with a reputation for poor quality. An experimental independent rear suspension allowed engineer John Z. De Lorean to see how low he could go. Advertisements announced the 'Wide Track Look' and publicity drawings exaggerated the proportions. This was the moment when width became sexy. Then De Lorean, who liked European sports cars, decided to insert a vast 5,178 cubic cm (316 cubic in) V-8 into the Tempest. The result was the preposterously fast GTO, named shamelessly after the Ferrari Gran Turismo Omologato. This was the start of the muscle-car craze.

1965

Toyota 2000GT

This, with the later Datsun 240Z, was a Japanese response to the Jaguar E-Type, which it closely resembles in proportion and general arrangement, if not in details. A source of both cars was early work by Albrecht Goertz for Yamaha, who eventually manufactured the sophisticated cylinder heads used on the truck engine used in the production version of this car. However, very few were actually made: just 337, including two used by the cinema version of James Bond in an early and influential example of product placement. It is, thus, that rarest of things: a limited edition Japanese product. The 2000GT was, at a time when Toyota was trying to establish itself in Western markets, evidence of the increasing confidence of the Japanese motor industry, although its design was wholly derivative of

European and American originals. Details include aero mirrors and a racing-style fuel cap (although at this time Toyota had no real record of competition success yet) and cute service doors, suggestive of deep, satisfying covert technology. The striking phallic morphology spoke an international language, although in the chrome, jewellery and bizarrely shaped orifices an original Japanese formal language is beginning to emerge.

1966

Oldsmobile Toronado

Errett Lobban Cord made the first giant American cars with front-wheel drive. Oldsmobile made the last. In fact, the 1966 Oldsmobile Toronado was the last great US car, irrespective of the traction system: the editors of *Consumer Guide* called it a 'landmark creation', but it is really more of a tombstone. The '66 Toronado (the name is a splendid example of General Motors' bizarre habit of mangling perfectly good words) began as 1962 sketches for a dream car known as 'The Red Renderings' by Oldsmobile's Assistant Chief Designer, David North. The Toronado is a superlatively transgressive technical concept, tightly wrapped in fuss-free sculpture of complete originality. The compact front-wheel-drive system did not seduce Oldsmobile into making a compact package: the Toronado had a wheel base of nearly 3m (10ft), the length of a Mini, and weighed 1,980kg (4,366lb). Yates explains that Oldsmobile engineers evaluated an E-Type, a Corvette, a Ferrari and a racing Porsche 904, but did not understand these cars, complaining about the noisy Jaguar and cramped Chevy. So they did something original instead. The styling is bold and simple: massively flared wheel arches create a motif in their own right and the C-posts of the pillarless coupé glide lasciviously into a fastback. Toronado was the last 'personal' car: soon afterwards US manufacturers lost their confidence in vulgar magnificence.

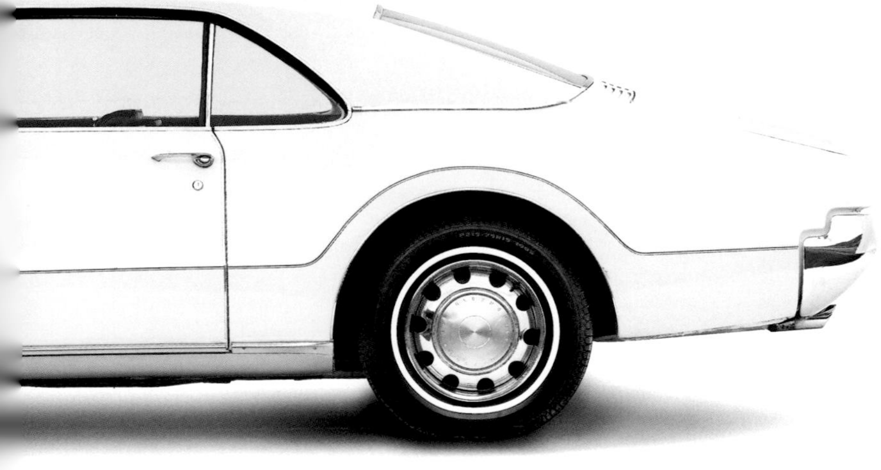

1966

Toyota Corolla

Plain of aspect and technologically unadventurous, the Toyota Corolla is the most successful car ever made. The perfect product of the Japanese industrial method (which has been called 'the machine that changed the world'), the 1966 Corolla is a demonstration of what can be achieved by the teamwork of subordinated egos instead of the bravura imaginings of the autonomous genius. From the day it was founded in 1931 by Kiichiro Toyoda, Toyota was committed to self-sufficiency. Accordingly, it established rigid disciplines and methodologies. As a result, while in 1956 annual Toyota production had been about 12,000 units, by 1970 it was comfortably over a million… most of them Corollas. The name 'Corolla' was first used in 1961 on one of Toyota's five domestic sales channels, established to sell a car called Publica. The sales channel and the car became the Corolla when the Publica name was dropped in 1966. In design terms it was an American car in miniature: chrome, white walls, shiny vinyl, a variety of body styles. The Sprinter coupé may have looked like a miniature Mustang, but at about 725kg (1,600lb) it weighed not much more than half as much.

1966

Volvo 144

There is a pathos about this car which maps the coordinates of Swedish design. The mid-Sixties, when it was launched, was the last moment of innocence for the Swedish design movement before the global success of IKEA turned social-democratic aesthetics into a tacky marketing phenomenon. Jan Wilsgaard began the design process in 1960, responding to a demanding management brief. Production cars were shown to the press in August 1966. The 144 carried Volvo styling cues, including the nostrils first seen on Wilsgaard's Amazon, but they are here reduced to vestigial motifs in the radiator brightwork. The 144 has a dignity and clarity that allowed the car to become a development platform for more than 20 years. It was the basis for Volvo's semantics of safety which, eventually, it turned into a house style. From simple rubber strip inserted into the bumpers, by the last models the 144 had acquired enormous protective apparatus front and rear. Other devices, including the energy-absorbing reverse slant nose, first went to market on the 144.

1966

Alfa Romeo Duetto Spider

In the *Lessico della carrozzeria* (1979), Pininfarina defines 'Spider' as 'La vettura sportive per eccelenza, generalamenta a 2 posti, con carrozzeria aperta e capote ripiegabile.' ('The sports car par excellence, generally two seats with open body-work and a folding hood.') The Alfa Spider was the company's first modern two-seater in the same way that the Ford Transit, introduced the same year, was Ford's first modern van. To publicize it Alfa held a competition to find a name. The winner was a Signor Guidobaldo Trionfi of Brescia with 'Duetto'. In May 1966 the first batch of Duettos was exported to the United States and the following year the car entered global folk memory when it was Dustin Hoffman's transport in Mike Nichols' *The Graduate*, a film that closed the generation gap with its slickly packaged and elegantly photographed transgenerational, sex. The design was by Pininfarina, with reflections of earlier experimental Alfas, especially the Disco Volante (or Flying Saucer) of 1955. The Duetto's tail was originally an elegant, curvaceous boatback or what the Italians call a '*coda di rospo*' (cuttlefish tail). This was changed in 1970 to a truncated rear, vaguely suggestive of the aerodynamic 'Kammheck', the sharply cut-off treatment advocated by Wunibald Kamm, wizard of aerodynamics. Not a lot about the Duetto was quite so scientific.

1967

NSU Ro80

It was Claus Luthe who designed the body of the most radically engineered production car ever. Development began in 1961 and it was launched at the Frankfurt Motor Show six years later: to avoid nagging questions of personal vanity, no design or engineering credits were given. So rumours began that this dramatic shape had been sculpted by Giacomo Manzu. Luthe, in his own words, aimed at 'sleekness and elegance'. The compact Wankel rotary engine allowed for the dramatic wedge shape, although Luthe's most radical ideas were compromised by production realities. Early proposals included versions with sliding doors. For instance, the front wheel arch looks too big for the tyre because at the last minute engineers insisted on changing the springs without allowing the designer to alter the radius of the arch. Engineers also altered the width of the car, compromising the purity of the designer's original idea. The Ro80 was intuitively aerodynamic: it first went into a wind-tunnel after the design was complete. The roof was intended to be brushed stainless steel, giving the glasshouse an appearance of immateriality. In April 1977 the last car left the Neckarsulm factory and the name NSU died.

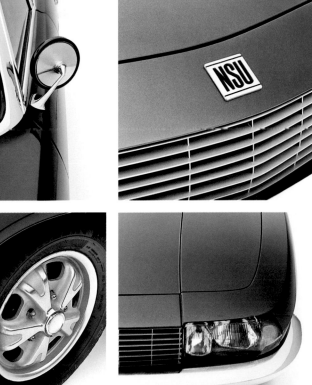

1967

Alfa Romeo Montreal

In terms of cultural reference, the astonishing Montreal was conceived in the year Sergeant Pepper was published; in terms of style, it is midway between the fashion eccentricities of Paco Rabanne (who thought women should wear frocks of plastic and aluminium) and the coming age of the first-generation pocket calculators. For the Montreal, Alfa adapted the V-8 engine of the successful T33 sports racing car, but mounted it in the front, giving the futuristic car a primeval phallomorphic profile. Despite its intergalactic allure, the rest of the Montreal was based on the humdrum 1750 saloon. Creative credits went to engineers Orazio Satta Puliga and Giuseppe Busso. Design credits went to Bertone as a whole, but specifically to Giorgetto Giugiaro and Marcello Gandini, rivals for the crown. The

Montreal, all voluptuous curves, evocative metal, slats and Plexiglass lenses, beautiful proportions and odd colours, was clearly – especially from the rear – inspired by Giugiaro's 1966 Miura for Lamborghini. The significance of the Montreal is as an attempt, on a budget, to commercialize the most extreme fantasies of the car designer. The advertisements said that it was a 'dream car come true'. On this occasion they were wrong. While consumer response to the show cars was near-hysterical, the Alfa Romeo reality failed to match the Alfa Romeo imagination and production ended in 1975 with fewer than 4,000 Montreals built.

1968

Ferrari Daytona

The Daytona was named, with an eye to the American market, after a famous victory in the 24-hour race at the Daytona Speedway in Florida in 1967 when three Ferrari racers crossed the line abreast. There is an American self-consciousness about the 365/GTB4, as it is correctly known. Although it is based on the harsher and more rudimentary GTB/4, the Daytona was bigger and softer. Significantly, most cars retained the signature wheels of the successful sports-racers: five-spoke alloy castings in a distinctive star pattern, usually painted gold. This is not the purest Ferrari, but it is one of the most significant. It is a Ferrari conceived not as racing car but a luxury product and it has styling to match. There are two unusual expressive elements: the concave side-moulding and the aero-nose which marked the (temporary) formal subjugation of the Ferrari frontal orifice. The Daytona was the last front-engined Berlinetta and the last Ferrari to be produced on the old studio/workshop system; Pininfarina would send a prototype to the Ferrari factory at Maranello. This would be reviewed by Ferrari himself, as well as by his dealers. After critical comments had been made and agreed, the car was handed over to master metal-basher Sergio Scaglietti, who would then make a limited edition of 'reproductions' of the original. In the early Seventies the Ferrari factory withdrew from sports-car racing and a vital connection to a creative source was lost.

1968

Jaguar XJ6

The XJ (for 'Experimental Jaguar') was the last car in which the handwriting of Sir William Lyons, the company's quixotic founder, can unambiguously be seen. Regularly cited as one of the most beautiful four-door cars ever made, it was the last Jaguar before the ugly miscegenations and brawls of failed industrial marriages compromised a unique spirit. The XJ4 programme began in 1964. There were pleasing details: symmetrical fuel tanks allowed the creation of a functional square boot and Dunlop's low-profile tyres allowed the car to make the most of the exceptional stance required by its exquisitely realized body. It was modern, although there were period details: the signature eyelids over the two pairs of headlamps were a sculptural detail that conferred great character, but they were not optimized for automated production and required an uneconomical number of processes. As soon as new owners sought 'value engineering' they were rationalized away. The XJ6 had a thin-pillared glasshouse and pronounced tumblehome. The rising hipline forward of the rear wheel arch is too subtle to be compared with the vulgarian 'Coca-Cola bottle curve' of contemporary Chevrolets and Pontiacs, instead conferring on the car something of the animal grace of its feral namesake.

1970

Citroën SM

The Citroën SM had a unique frontal aspect as well as a number of other unique aspects, many of them less happily resolved. Conceived as the (illogical) development of the 1955 DS, the SM achieved more notoriety than celebrity, because the creative ambition of its manufacturers so far exceeded their practical abilities. The number plate behind glass is a defining detail that was borrowed from a prototype of Claus Luthe's NSU Ro80, spied when Citroën and NSU were collaborating on the Comotor project to share the technology of the Wankel rotary engine. This had its origins in Citroën's historic dissatisfaction at never having fitted the old Goddess with an engine as fine as the rest of the car. But the engine's shortcomings perplexed even the saintly, and the strange SM was the product of another and even more unlikely collaboration… with Maserati (which Citroën had, somewhat idiosyncratically, acquired in 1968). SM in fact stands for 'Serie Maserati'. Curious details include asymmetric seating and the world's first injection-moulded GRP (glass reinforced plastic) wheels. The lascivious body was drawn by Robert Opron and built by Henri Chapron. The SM appears a miracle of integrated shapemaking. While a Seventies Aston Martin is all difficult angles and two dimensions, the SM is magnificently sculpted: the total expression of a unique formal idea.

1970

Range Rover

Its origins were in a Fifties concept of 'Road Rover', a hybrid agricultural vehicle and saloon car, but the Range Rover went further: a perfect psychographic representation of the aspirations of the market sector it established. Later, like all good designs, it showed itself capable of development and turned into various mutations. Engineers Spen King and Gordon Bashford with designer David Bache began work on the Range Rover in 1967. They ignored an axiom and produced a design that did not take time to acquire brand values, but had them from the start. Signature design features included a roof that appears to float above black-painted pillars, a clam shell bonnet and 'castellations' which offered the driver an automotive version of a weapon's sights. It was functionality turned into design language. A mass of features had a profound effect on the customer's perceptions of this exciting new product. Interior details were elegantly modern and conceived to be modular. There was a hose-down plastic interior. Originally, the concept was felt to be so correct, that there was a single model with a single specification.

1971

Alfasud

Alfasud began in 1968, a project by the then state-owned Alfa Romeo to have a car suitable for production in the Mezzogiorno, the troubled south of the country with criminal and agricultural rather than industrial and manufacturing traditions. The engineer responsible for the Alfasud was Rudolf Hruska, a one-time collaborator with Ferdinand Porsche. But his concern here was packaging. Space utilization was exceptional: of an overall 3.96m (13ft) length, 2.8m (9ft 2in) are for passengers and luggage. His boxer engine has clear Porsche heredity, but allows a short and low nose. It was placed ahead of the front axle so the interior is not compromised by any intrusions. Giorgetto Giugiaro of ItalDesign in Moncalieri, near Turin, was commissioned to design the body. It was his first mass-market project. Hruska presented a tight dimensional brief and the demand for high visibility meant a low

beltline and large glasshouse were inevitable. Doors make maximum possible use of the space between the wheels. Giugiaro placed the windscreen well forward, an effect that only emphasizes the large passenger cell. At the rear a fastback descends to a vertical tail. The Alfasud had an exceptionally low drag coefficient of 0.30.

1971

FIAT 130 Coupé

There may be no such car as a 'Pininfarina', but the big FIAT coupé of 1972 comes close. This was a version of the FIAT 130, a premium-priced large car that was a misplaced expression of confidence by a company that made its reputation out of economy and moderation. The saloon was designed by FIAT's in-house Centro Stile. Giacosa directed his team not to ape the timelessness of Mercedes-Benz, but to aim for more American effects. He had misgivings, since his heart was in the design of small cars with all the intellectual economy and material parsimony a modest budget imposed. As a result, the 1969 130 saloon was not well born. The design of the Coupé was given to Pininfarina

and the car appeared at the 1972 Geneva Salon. Confidently undecorated, razor-edged, imposing, glassy and elegant, it was the final expression of one Italian tradition. Later that year, an exhibition at New York's Museum of Modern Art called 'Italy: The New Domestic Landscape' set a new schema for Italian design and set the agenda for a new generation who had a decided antipathy to the car.

1971

Lamborghini Countach

The plan view of a Lamborghini Countach makes it clear that it is, conceptually speaking, an origami graphic of other-worldly outrage, made not of Japanese paper, but of aircraft-grade aluminium. The prototype, known as Project 112, was shown at the Geneva Salon de l'Automobile in 1971. The 10-year gap since the Jaguar E-Type allowed the public to accumulate reserves of astonishment, all spent on viewing this car. The Countach was designed by Marcello Gandini, who took the seat left empty at Carrozzeria Bertone when Giorgetto Giugiaro set up on his own in 1965. Gandini's style combines aggressive angularity and dramatic proportions with a sublime refusal to consider practicalities. The

signature scissor doors were required because conventional openings were not practicable on this imponderably wide car. Challenges to functionality included negligible rear vision, not much aided by a periscope rear-view mirror. The passenger cab is placed well forward and inside there are period-style digital instruments. The car is only 1m (3ft 6in) tall. 'Countach' is Piedmontese *voce de gergo*, the gasp of astonishment made, for example, on sight of an exceptionally attractive woman. The car was manufactured from 1974 to 1990 and established the category of 'supercar'. The Countach is the definitive supercar: a shape so dramatic that it still astonishes more than 35 years later.

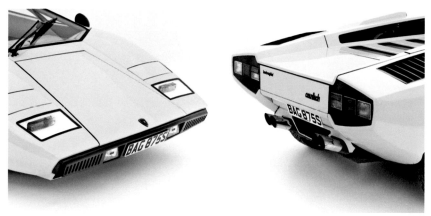

1972

BMW 5 Series

1972 was the year of the Olympics in Munich. It was a moment of optimism for both Germany and BMW. BMW built a headquarters building inspired by the shape of an internal combustion engine and next to it BMW-Welt, a theatre where corporate values were put on the stage. The 1972 5 Series was the protagonist. The designer was Frenchman Paul Bracq, who had earlier worked on the Mercedes-Benz 300SL, and would later work on Alstom's Train à Grande Vitesse for the Société Nationale des Chemins de Fer. He became Design Director of BMW in 1970. For the new Fünfer, Bracq used the design language established by Willhelm Hofmeister, adapted to a contemporary package: twin headlights in a full-width black grille, crisp graphics with a prominent beltline, emphatic

jewellery, a masculine stance with feminine details and radii. And then there was a big glasshouse. A German critic complained that glass is heavier, more expensive and more dangerous than metal. But the critic was ignored. The success of the Fünfer showed consumer choices are emotional, not rational. The 5 Series offered a synecdoche of middle-class values, setting a design standard effectively unaltered for a quarter of a century.

1972

Renault 5

Although the word did not exist at the time, this was the first modern hatchback. The Renault 5, although based on the very dated running gear of the R4, was a radical innovation in car architecture: to a package as neat as the Mini, it added French style, a hatchback and the signature polyester wraparound bumpers (a world first). It was designed by Michel Boué who died, aged 35, before the car's commercial debut in 1972. While the British Mini had utilitarian charm, the French R5 had urban chic. Boué's sculpture was wholly original: there were large areas of shockingly plain metal and generous glazing. An uncompromisingly plain nose and a preponderance of vertical and near-vertical lines gave the car an attractively alert aspect. There were some notably architectural details, too: handles were cleverly integrated into the trailing edge of the door and the interior was frankly addressed to an audience not yet debauched by the fripperies of postmodernism: it was stark, but clever. Originally Boué proposed rear lights running the entire length of the C-pillar. This

motif, which later became an industry cliché, was rejected on grounds of cost. Media promotion was intense and the car embarrassingly anthropomorphized in advertisements shown in 268 Paris and 1,446 provincial cinemas, where it appeared as a cute person. The Publicis advertising agency directed communications towards women, students and other '*étrangers*'. Whether or not the delightful R5 threatened conventional French conceptions of masculinity, it immediately took 5.8 per cent of the French market.

1974

Volkswagen Golf

The Golf was a German take on Alec Issigonis' Mini formula, but with more precision and harder edges. The body was based on designs by the great Giorgetto Giugiaro. Giugiaro's first car for ItalDesign was the Alfasud, his second the Golf, one of the most significant cars of all time. The Golf is almost entirely comprised of straight lines and flat panels, but the effect was not one of tectonic crudeness, rather of breathtaking novelty. Early Golfs were astonishingly minimal: drivers sat upright on hard, vertical seats with very few concessions to comfort, let alone luxury. Instruments were in a single pod and inside was hard, shiny plastic. Giugiaro helped Volkswagen to create an intensely desirable product. Its generous glass areas added daylight to a thrilling sense of freshness. The Golf's style was criticized by some as ham-fisted industrial origami, but it is a sharp-edged box of great subtlety. More significantly, while the straight lines were an expression of Giugiaro's aesthetic, they also served notice that Volkswagen was reborn: the Beetle's period curves and radii were emphatically replaced by modern linear geometry.

1977

SAAB 99 Turbo

Drawings from the mid-Fifties by designer Sixten Sason predict the general arrangement of the 99: a truncated tail, a nose-down attitude and a big glasshouse with low waistline. One version shows dramatic glazing: SAAB 99s are unique in having a windscreen that is almost semi-circular in plan. A prototype in the SAAB Museum in Trollhattan built in the mid-Sixties (when the design was being established) shows how SAAB's thinking was evolving: the car was to be a big Swedish Mini. Sason was assisted in the studio by an English architect, Peter Maddock, and his protégé, Bjorn Envall. It was Envall who led the team that turned the humdrum 99 into the 1977 Turbo. Bjorn Envall gave it a design language. The original two-door 99 was turned into a more interesting hatchback called the 900. Envall wanted to achieve stand-out for a new, fast, technologically interesting car. He put a spoiler beneath the rear window. He designed alloy wheels that created a stroboscopic effect on the move. Most were specified in dramatic black paint, and Envall made vents and jewellery emphatic.

1979

FIAT Panda

The Panda was not just designed by an external consultancy, but worked up to a fully engineered package ready for manufacture. The consultancy was ItalDesign, founded by Giorgetto Giugiaro, the greatest Italian car designer after Pininfarina. In offering not just agreeable body design, but an entire viable package, Giugiaro distanced himself from the old *carrozzerie*. His opportunity with the Panda was to establish himself as the most innovative, yet practical, designer. With the Panda Giugiaro wanted to make an intelligent utilitarianism chic. He broke strict industry taboos and made a virtue of asymmetry with its off-centre air intake. He wanted to make economy explicit and used flat glass (which by the Law of Unintended Consequences actually made production more expensive). Proportioned to fit into narrow alleys in Italian hill towns, the Panda was given boldly expressive polypropylene impact protection that occupied nearly a third of the car's surface area. Metal panels were uncomplicated pressings. Inside, the modular instrument panel could be quickly adapted to either left- or right-hand drive. There was enormous internal storage space and a striking simplicity. Like the Citroën deux chevaux which it conceptually resembles,

hammock-type seats could be removed and there was a single windscreen wiper. The Panda was the first car to be more of a product design than an automobile, and established Giugiaro as the pre-eminent consultant designer. For his part, he said that it was his most complete design.

1982

Ford Sierra

Finding a successor to the Cortina tested Ford's marketing genius and its nerve. With aerodynamics and safety influencing auto industry designers, the Sierra was a demonstration of the public understanding of science. The science is straightforward: at speeds above a mere 60kp/h (37mph), aerodynamic drag absorbs more energy than rolling resistance. Drag is represented by CD, a calculation that gives an open parachute a CD of 1.35 and a pure aerofoil section a CD of 0.05. An efficient saloon car aims at 0.35. This was Ford's target with the radical Sierra, a mass-market product designed to persuade the public of the status value of efficient penetration. The public read it differently and tabloids soon spoke derisively of a 'jelly mould'. The Sierra was designed by a team led by Uwe Bahnsen. When the Sierra was tested (without identifying badges) in consumer clinics, a majority felt that it was more expensive than the $2,000 target price. But the research did not ask the consumers if they would actually buy it. The Sierra enhanced Ford's reputation among sophisticates, but its cool commercial reception alarmed management and sent Ford back to a conservative design policy that lasted 20 years.

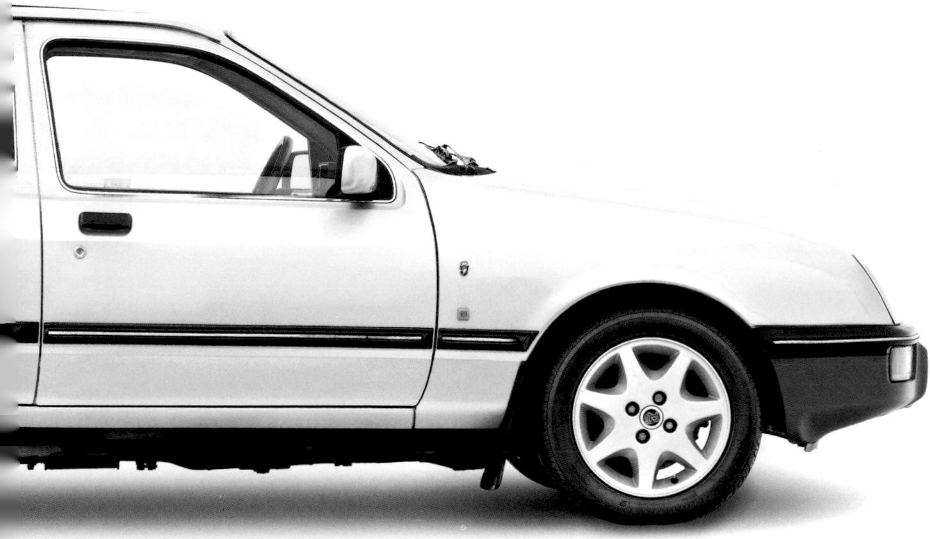

1982

Audi 100

Only slowly did Audi achieve a design integrity independent of its Volkswagen master, which bought the company in 1965. When Ferdinand Piëch, grandson of Dr Porsche, took control he determined to establish a new identity with a series of audacious 'technical events'. The 1982 Audi 100 was a tipping point for Audi's credibility. Exploiting creative cues established in experimental safety cars in the Seventies, the Audi 100 appeared at the very moment when marketers had determined that explicit technology would give the product a USP, a Unique Selling Proposition. The 100 was sheer and streamlined: superlatively made, an enormous but light and elegant body covered advanced componentry. The windows carried pegs which ran in slides, providing nearly flush glazing. In addition, the 100, with its confidently sheer surfaces and overt functional intelligence, established an Audi design language that lasted a quarter of a century. Its drag coefficient was 0.30. To emphasize its essential German character, the advertising agency Bartle Bogle Hegarty wrote the ineffable Eighties copyline 'Vorsprung durch Technik' and gave Audi brand values whose appeal had a near-erotic intensity for the new money of the decade.

1992

Renault Twingo

At Renault, Patrick Le Quément persuaded Raymond Levy that research showing 25 per cent of respondents disliked the Twingo concept should be ignored. In time, the Twingo changed popular conception of the small car: it was, in a phallo-centric world, gender-neutral and in its design Le Quément bravely played with the symbolism and palette of the toy box. The Twingo jumped the species barrier and became an enjoyable product, rather than a prosthetic sexual device. 'As designers, we are in a fight between sheer seduction and image building,' Le Quément explained. 'A design statement that brings immediate returns but does not build the brand is a mistake.' The Twingo was launched at the Paris Salon of 1992; simultaneously, Renault refreshed its corporate graphics. Instrumentation was minimal, clutter eschewed. Rear seats slid and the package was gasp-making: a foot shorter than the Clio, the Twingo had more space than a Renault 25. The price was kept down (to 55,000FR) because the only option was colour. Le Quément was characteristically contrarian: at a time when white was the most popular colour for French cars, the Twingo was not available in it. Instead, the palette included green, purple, bubble-gum pink and brown. Despite its celebrity, the Twingo was never taken up by youth: it was a strange example of radical design appealing to the middle-aged.

1998

smart

In 1994 Daimler-Benz and Swatch, the novelty watch manufacturer, announced a joint venture to produce a car. This rich and bizarre concatenation of influences created the first car to establish a new format since the Mini. Early development was in California, under a team led by Gerhard Steinle. Rolled out on 2 October 1998 with an overall length of 2.5m (8ft), smart was promoted as a new urban transport system. The architecture was defined by an ultra-strong and visually emphatic steel frame with eco-friendly powder paint. Panels were made of recycled plastic, easily replaced. The packaging was extraordinary: a tiny three-cylinder engine mounted below floor level at the rear allowed accommodation for two passengers with similar space and amenity to a mid-sized saloon. Consumers were at first perturbed, especially as early models had stability problems (caused by a very short wheelbase and a very high centre of gravity). But eventually the extraordinary convenience and charm of the car won sceptics over. Consumers enjoyed its strange mixture of eccentricity and very high levels of physical quality. Both practically and artistically, a new language was established.

1999

Renault Avantime

The Avantime was shown as a concept at the Geneva Salon of 1999. Its purpose was to demonstrate, against the background of somewhat staid reality, Renault's culture of innovation. Its aim was no less than to redefine the architecture of the car for the new millennium. Proportions are curious: a single volume with thrusting snout at the front, a pert bottom at the rear. The rear window is vertical in side elevation but rounded in plan, helping to achieve a sense of dynamism, if not positive aesthetic unease. Large wheels gave the car an imposing stance, but it was the apertures that made the car remarkable. All the side glass in this pillarless coupé with a full-length glass roof retracted. Exceptionally large doors travelled on a twin-stage mechanism making access easy but minimizing the arc of travel. Inside, the furnishings were four imponderably large chairs, as if in an avant-garde Bentley. The Avantime went into production in 2001 but it was not, according to Renault's Patrick Le Quément, 'well born'. Problems in manufacturing a demanding specification led to

delays and, in turn, these led to quality problems experienced by the few customers bold enough to bet on a concept. Despite, or perhaps because of, its outstandingly innovative character, the Avantime was a commercial failure: sorry evidence that it is not prudent to test Raymond Loewy's principle of MAYA ('most advanced yet acceptable').

2002

Nissan Cube

Shiro Nakamura, Nissan's Chief Designer, has said, 'It is our task to ask how to make the car more exciting, more expressive and more attractive.' So he designed a car apparently modelled on a paediatric psychologist's Froebel block. The overture to the Cube was the Chapeau concept of 1989 and the Chappo concept car, first seen at the Geneva Salon de l'Automobile in 2001. Nakamura cites a strong inspirational link to the formalism of traditional Japanese culture, but the Cube also draws on more recent and frequently eccentric Japanese design traditions. Nissan has a happy tradition of specializing in high-concept, low-volume genre cars with a retro-futuristic feel: the Be-1 of 1985, the S-Cargo of 1987 and the Figaro of 1989, all the products of a consultant 'conceptor', each one a shock to the system and an amusing affront to convention. The Cube is a development of these experiments. The Japanese have no very great tradition of sculpture in the round but excel at graphics. The Cube is like a diagram composed of straight lines and right angles, mediated by understated and disciplined curves. It is odd, uncompromising, innovative and exceptionally efficient in terms of space utilization.

2003

BMW 5

BMW's traditional refusal of change demonstrated an essential belief in the rightness of its design, established nearly 40 years ago by Paul Bracq. In this way, BMW told its customers they were doing the right thing: buying a BMW was like joining an evangelical sect which worshipped handsome and understated design. In 2003 BMW decided on radical change. In the world of car design, this was a disruption that may be compared to Picasso's creation of Cubism. The new design direction, originally described as 'flame surfacing', was controversial: in place of good proportions there is imbalance; thoughtful details have been replaced by baroque flourishes; a sense of rationality has been usurped by wilful expressiveness; calm sobriety has been blinded and deafened by a taste for tactile instability and graphic fidgetiness. While this alienated many established customers, it was partly justified by changing demographics; Chinese and Indian markets are less tolerant of BMW's gentility. Chris Bangle says, 'It is the most avant-garde thing BMW has ever done. When that thing is in front of me, I just want to follow it.'

Were an Alien Visitor
To hover a few hundred yards above the planet
It could be forgiven for thinking
That cars were the dominant life-form,
And that human beings were a kind of ambulatory fuel cell,
Injected when the car wished to move off,
And ejected when they were spent.

Heathcote Williams, 1991

Acknowledgements

PAGE 202–205

Cadillac Eldorado Biarritz
Mark & Pip Sumpter
www.paragon.gb.com

PAGE 206–209

Lincoln Continental
Ciaran Payne

PAGE 210–213

Jaguar E-Type
John Creed Miles

PAGE 214–217

BMW 1500
BMW

PAGE 218–221

NSU Prinz
Rob Talbot

PAGE 222–225

Alfa Romeo Giulia
Jeremy Brown

PAGE 226–229

Renault 4
Tim Jackson

PAGE 230–233

Lancia Flavia Zagato
Bill Amberg

PAGE 234–237

Ford Cortina
Brain Raymond

PAGE 238–241

Porsche 911
Maxted Page
www.maxted-page.com

PAGE 242–245

Buick Riviera
Classic Car Club
www.classiccarclub.co.uk

PAGE 246–249

Rover P6
Nick Dunning

PAGE 250–253

Mercedes-Benz SL
Classic Chrome Ltd
www.classic-chrome.co.uk

PAGE 254–257

Chevrolet Corvette
Pat Fitzgerald

PAGE 258–261

Panhard 24CT
Brian Oswald

PAGE 262–265

Ferrari 250GTO
Nick Mason

PAGE 266–269

Ford Mustang
Classic Car Club
www.classiccarclub.co.uk

PAGE 270–273

Pontiac GTO
Tim Arrowsmith

PAGE 274–277

Toyota 2000GT
Robert Close

PAGE 278–281

Oldsmobile Toronado
Spurr Cars
www.americancarsuk.com

PAGE 282–285

Toyota Corolla
Dave Dawson

PAGE 286–289

Volvo 144
Gillian Whitton

PAGE 290–293

Alfa Romeo Duetto Spider
Richard Rees

PAGE 294–297

NSU Ro80
Vincent Demarest

PAGE 298–301

Alfa Romeo Montreal
Rob Jones

PAGE 302–305

Ferrari Daytona
DK Engineering
www.dkeng.co.uk

PAGE 306–309

Jaguar XJ6
Paul Duce
www.classics-cabriolets.co.uk

PAGE 310–313

Citroën SM
Paul Duce
www.classics-cabriolets.co.uk

PAGE 314–317
Range Rover
Richard Beddall

PAGE 318–321
Alfasud
Stephen Butler

PAGE 322–325
FIAT 130 Coupé
Paul Duce
www.classics-cabriolets.co.uk

PAGE 326–329
Lamborghini Countach
Stephen Ward

PAGE 330–333
BMW 5 Series
BMW

PAGE 334–337
Renault 5
Ian Seabrook

PAGE 338–341
Volkswagen Golf
Volkswagen

PAGE 342–345
SAAB 99 Turbo
Brian Bergin

PAGE 346–349
Fiat Panda
Samantha Wakes
Michael English

PAGE 350–353
Ford Sierra
Paul D Elliot

PAGE 354–357
Audi 100
Audi UK

PAGE 358–361
Renault Twingo
Tim Eager

PAGE 362–365
smart
Cool Cars 4 Hire Limited

PAGE 366–369
Renault Avantime
Stephen Dell

PAGE 370–373
Nissan Cube
Red Line Imports
www.redlineimports.co.uk

PAGE 374–377
BMW 5
BMW

The publisher would like to thank the following contributors for their kind permission to reproduce the photographs in this book.

10 Fonds Doisneau/ Collection Renault, France;13 below 6487/Gamma/ Camera Press London; 14 Sanford H.Roth/Seita Ohnishi/Rapho/ Camera Press London;15 Louis Faurer, Courtesy of Mark Faurer;16 left Rossi-Siochan/ Gamma/Camera Press London; 16 right Zoltan Glass/NMeM/Science & Society Picture Library;17 left Michael Ormerod/ Millennium Images; 17 right Zoltan Glass/NMeM/ Science & Society Picture Library;18 above ©2008 Digital Image, The Museum of Modern Art, New York/Scala, Florence; 18 below CarCulture/Getty Images;21 Aerialarchives.com /Alamy;22 Keystone-France/ Camera Press London; 23 Keystone-France/Camera Press London;24 Pininfarina; 24 below Elliott Erwitt/ Magnum Photos;26 left Car Culture/Getty Images;26 right Jacques Henri Lartigue ©Ministere de la Culture, France/AAJHL;27 left Pierre Belzeaux/ Rapho/ Camera Press London;27 right Farrenkopf/BMW AG Konzernarchiv;28 Three Lions/Getty Images;29 ©2008. Digital Image, The Museum of Modern Art, New York/Scala, Florence;31 ©Walker Evans Archive, The Metropolitan Museum of Art (1994.251.482 Auto Graveyard in Field, 1933, Film negative $2^1/2$ x $4^1/4$ in.)

Every effort has been made to trace the copyright holders. We apologize in advance for any unintentional omissions and would be pleased to insert the appropriate acknowledgement in any subsequent publication.

The author would like to thank…

All books are collaborative exercises, this one more so than most. First I must thank Tom Wolfe whose *The Kandy-Kolored Tangerine-Flake Streamline Baby* I read on my knee beneath a desk in school forty years ago. The book, like Tom himself, still inspires me. Indeed, it inspired our title, as textual sleuths will have noted. Next, the editorial, production and picture research team at Conran Octopus. Lorraine Dickey, Sybella Marlow, Sian Parkhouse and Anne-Marie Hoines were always exceptionally supportive, charming and efficient, even when nagging. Extra special thanks, however, to Katherine Hockley who handled a very complicated production without complaint. At least, without complaint to me! Jonathan Christie's superb design has made *Cars* even better than I hoped it would be. But the very special character of this book is due to Tif Hunter. His photographs utterly transcend the limitations of a sometimes trashy medium: Tif's pictures alone make the case for cars as works of art. And all of them were made possible by an ingenious travelling studio of Tif's own invention. But had it not been for Tif's indefatigable agent and producer, Sue Allatt, we would have had nothing to photograph. With very unusual and cheerful persistence, Sue found cars in sheds, airport hangars and suburban garages. She patiently negotiated access with all the owners who were, of course, the most important collaborators of all.

The photographer would like to thank…

In my case the debt of inspiration comes from one of my long-time photographic heroes, Irving Penn. With his book *Worlds in a Small Room*, he shot people from far-flung places in situ using a tent with a plain background. The design and fabrication of my tent was brilliantly executed by Andy Knight and Pete Jenkins. It performed brilliantly and coped without a hitch despite all that the English weather threw at it. The erection of said tent, car cleaning and all the other photography-related duties were ably carried out by a team of assistants that included Jared Price, Dave Mitchell, Scott MacSween, Jasper Hunter, Emma Tunbridge, Enda Bowe, John Wilson, Liz McBurney, Tom East, Klaus Madengruber, Stuart Hendry, Fraser Lawson, Tom Andrew, Graham Wardale, Luke aan de Weil and Joe Giacomet. My agent, Sue Allatt, deserves a medal for sourcing all the cars and I know she would like to thank Mike Hallowes of Ten Tenths for his invaluable knowledge and assistance. I'd also like to thank Jonathan Christie from Conran Octopus for asking me to be involved in this project in the first place. To see and touch such an array of beautiful cars and to meet their owners has been a pleasure and a privilege.

The publisher would like to thank…

Peter Jones (www.fiatpandaclub.co.uk), Billy Roe (www.northamericanmotorco.com), The boys at Classic Car Club (www.classiccarclub.co.uk), Andy Craig at *Classic American* magazine (www.classic-american.com), Savo at Clerkenwell Motors (www.clerkenwellmotors.co.uk), Ted Bemand, RM Auctions (www.rmauctions.com), Arthur & Elieen Melrose, The Historic VW Club, Gavin Ward at BMW, Audi UK, Volkswagen, Julian Balme, Robert Coucher at *Octane* magazine, Ricky James, Eddy Pearce, Foxy, South Western Vehicle Auctions, Pontiac Drivers Club, Yorkshire Motor Musum.